TRAUMA INFORMED GUILT REDUCTION THERAPY

TRAUMA INFORMED GUILT REDUCTION THERAPY

Treating Guilt and Shame Resulting from Trauma and Moral Injury

SONYA NORMAN
University of California, San Diego, CA, United States

CAROLYN ALLARD
Alliant International University, San Diego, CA, United States

KENDALL BROWNE
University of Washington, Seattle, WA, United States

CHRISTY CAPONE
Brown University, Providence, RI, United States

BRITTANY DAVIS
University of South Florida, Tampa, FL, United States

EDWARD KUBANY
Honolulu, HI, United States

ELSEVIER

ACADEMIC PRESS
An imprint of Elsevier

Academic Press is an imprint of Elsevier
125 London Wall, London EC2Y 5AS, United Kingdom
525 B Street, Suite 1650, San Diego, CA 92101, United States
50 Hampshire Street, 5th Floor, Cambridge, MA 02139, United States
The Boulevard, Langford Lane, Kidlington, Oxford OX5 1GB, United Kingdom

Library of Congress Cataloging-in-Publication Data
A catalog record for this book is available from the Library of Congress

British Library Cataloguing-in-Publication Data
A catalogue record for this book is available from the British Library

ISBN 978-0-12-814780-1

For information on all Academic Press publications visit our website at https://www.elsevier.com/books-and-journals

Publisher: Nikki Levy
Acquisition Editor: Dennis McGonagle
Editorial Project Manager: Megan Ashdown
Production Project Manager: Vijayaraj Purushothaman
Cover Designer: Miles Hitchen

Typeset by SPi Global, India

Contents

Bios

Sonya Norman, Ph.D., received her B.A. from Vassar College in cultural anthropology and her Ph.D. in counseling psychology from Stanford University. She is a professor of Psychiatry at the University of California San Diego School of Medicine and director of the PTSD Consultation Program at the VA's National Center for PTSD. She previously directed a PTSD treatment program for Veterans who served in Iraq and Afghanistan. She conducts research in treating posttraumatic guilt, shame, and moral injury as well as in the treatment of PTSD and addictions. She is passionate about bringing together clinical work and research. She has served as a training director for a postdoctoral fellowship in evidence-based psychotherapy. She has had research grants funded by the National Institute of Health, the Department of Defense, and the VA and has over 100 publications related to posttraumatic guilt and shame, PTSD, and associated problems.

Carolyn B. Allard, Ph.D., ABPP, received her B.A. (Hons.) from Queen's University in Kingston, Canada, and her Ph.D. in clinical psychology from the University of Oregon in Eugene, USA. She is a licensed and board certified clinical psychologist who has served as a director of the Veterans Affairs San Diego Healthcare System Military Sexual Trauma & Interpersonal Trauma Clinic and Advanced Fellowship in Women's Health, an associate professor of Psychiatry at University of California San Diego, and a clinical director of a private-sector residential mental health program. She currently is the Ph.D. program director at the California School of Professional Psychology at Alliant International University and has a private practice. For over 20 years, she has worked with survivors of many different types of trauma and specializes in the treatment of complex posttraumatic reactions to chronic and severe interpersonal trauma, including PTSD, dissociation, and guilt and shame. She has trained hundreds in working with trauma survivors, from entry level students to seasoned professionals, and she is an active trauma researcher who has published articles in several scientific journals.

Kendall Browne, Ph.D., earned her Ph.D. from the San Diego State University/University of California, San Diego Joint Doctoral Program in Clinical Psychology. She is currently a licensed psychologist and core faculty member within the VA Centers of Excellence in Substance Addiction Treatment and Education and an Acting Assistant Professor in the Department of Psychiatry and Behavioral Sciences within the University of Washington, School of Medicine. She has training and expertise in the assessment and treatment of substance use disorders and co-occurring trauma-related symptoms. Her research efforts to date have largely focused on developing and evaluating evidence-based practices for substance use disorders and co-occurring posttraumatic stress disorder.

Christy Capone, Ph.D., is a licensed, clinical psychologist with the Department of Veterans Affairs in Providence, RI. She is an assistant professor of Psychiatry and Human Behavior at the Warren Alpert School of Medicine at Brown University. Dr. Capone works with military Veterans in the Trauma Recovery Services clinic at the VA where she provides individual and group psychotherapy related to co-occurring posttraumatic stress disorder and substance use. She serves as a clinical supervisor and research mentor to psychology and psychiatry residents who are learning to deliver evidence-based psychotherapies and conduct clinical research. Informed by her clinical work with Veterans, Dr. Capone became interested in how to best address trauma-related guilt and shame, a problem that arose again and again in therapy and for many clients presented a formidable barrier to wellness and recovery. Her research interests have focused on this area for the past several years and she currently has a research grant funded by the Department of Defense. Dr. Capone also conducts research in novel treatments for co-occurring PTSD and substance use and has published several manuscripts in this area.

Brittany Davis, Ph.D., received her Ph.D. in clinical psychology from the California School of Professional Psychology at Alliant International University. She is a licensed clinical psychologist with the Department of Veterans Affairs in Tampa, Florida and is an assistant professor at the University of South Florida's Department of Psychiatry and Behavioral Neurosciences. She values training and education and has served as a clinical supervisor for psychology and psychiatry residents. She has remained active in research with a focus on trauma-related disorders, guilt and shame, and substance use disorders. She specializes in the treatment of PTSD and comorbid substance use disorders, and has utilized treatment approaches with flexibility and creativity, to assist with active duty service members, first responders, and Veterans within inpatient, residential, and outpatient settings. She works collaboratively with her clients and believes that if willing, all individuals have the capacity and capability to successfully overcome the distress of difficult times that may occur within the lifetime.

Edward Kubany, Ph.D., ABPP specialized in the assessment and treatment of PTSD and posttraumatic guilt in his research and clinical practice for close to 40 years. He was a research clinical psychologist with the Department of Veterans Affairs, National Center for PTSD, in Honolulu, Hawaii for 14 years. He has numerous peer-reviewed publications and was principle investigator or co-principal investigator on four federal grants. He is the first author of a self-help book for women who survived interpersonal violence, Healing the Trauma of Domestic Violence, and a clinician guide, Treating PTSD in Battered Women. He was on the forefront of bringing attention to the role of posttraumatic guilt in PTSD and posttraumatic distress as early as the 1990s. He developed measures and intervention strategies for posttraumatic guilt that are widely used to this day. His work in understanding posttraumatic guilt and in intervention strategies was critical to the development of TrIGR.

Acknowledgments

Sonya Norman
For my boys, Greg, Max, and Jack, who bring me joy every day. For my parents, Vladimir and Larisa, who taught me by example to never let fear get in my way. To my family in California, New York, Connecticut, and beyond for their love and support. Finally, for my DMH friends and workout buddies and all of the women who bring endless wisdom and much needed balance to my life.

Carolyn Allard
For my children, Tiegue and Cohen, and my parents, Jean-Louis and Rickie, who have contributed to this book more than they will ever know.

Kendall Browne
To my husband Tim, for his endless support and love. To my daughter Elliot, you are the light of my life. To my parents and siblings, whose love and encouragement created the foundation for all that I have achieved. To the inspiring and thriving women that I am lucky enough to call family, friends, and colleagues, your wisdom is a gift.

Christy Capone
For my fellas, Bob and Aidan, for all of the love and laughter. And for my parents, Robert and Dolores Capone, who taught me to aim higher and to have fun along the way.

Brittany Davis
For my son Quinn, who brings more joy than I could have ever imagined. For my husband, Benny for your continued encouragement. For Susan, for giving me a chance and pushing me in the right direction. Lastly, for my friends and family, near and far, for all your love and support.

Group acknowledgement (from all authors)

Roxy, thank you for giving your time and skill to make this book better. We would like to thank the many clients over the years who trusted us with their stories and allowed us to be part of their journey of healing from guilt and shame. We are honored and humbled by your courage. We also thank our colleagues and the many therapists from around the United States and abroad who have reached out to learn TrIGR and who have provided invaluable feedback on this therapy. This book would not be possible without all of you.

PART 1

Introduction and background

PART 1 INTRODUCTION AND BACKGROUND

CHAPTER 1

Introduction

Thank you for your interest in Trauma Informed Guilt Reduction (TrIGR) therapy! Before delving into TrIGR, we wanted to say a little about how TrIGR came to be. We saw the need for TrIGR in the course of our work as psychologists who specialize in treating trauma and posttraumatic stress disorder (PTSD). We have worked across different settings including general mental health, women's mental health, and outpatient and intensive/residential specialty PTSD treatment programs. We have treated survivors of many different kinds of trauma such as sexual assaults, intimate partner violence, motor vehicle accidents, and wars. Across all of these settings and trauma types, we saw one thing over and over again: people whose suffering stemmed from something they believed they did wrong before, during, or after the trauma. Sometimes the event they were suffering over was something they had done, like crashing into another car, missing warning signs from someone who turned out to be a rapist, exposing children to an abusive relationship, or firing a weapon in combat under unclear circumstances. Sometimes it was something they did not do, like saying no during a sexual assault or freezing instead of firing a weapon in combat. Regardless of the circumstances, what we saw as a result looked very similar. Guilt and shame over these events were causing a tremendous amount of pain and impairment in our clients' lives. Our clients were having problems in their relationships, as parents, and with their work. Many experienced moral injury, a type of trauma that involves a violation of deeply held morals and values that is characterized by strong guilt and shame reactions (Frankfurt & Frazier, 2016; Jinkerson, 2016; Litz et al., 2009). Many of our clients who experienced guilt and shame were depressed, had PTSD, or were using alcohol or drugs to cope with the situation. Some were suicidal. None were living the kind of life they wanted. We found that not all of these clients had PTSD and among those who did, some did not respond

Trauma Informed Guilt Reduction Therapy
https://doi.org/10.1016/B978-0-12-814780-1.00001-0

to PTSD treatments. It was difficult to help them recover from their pain and, as we got deeper into our work, we discovered one potential reason why—many did not believe they deserved to feel better because of what they had done wrong. Over and over we heard statements from our clients like "If I didn't feel bad because of what I did, then I would really be a monster," "I don't deserve to be loved," "If people knew what I did, they would want nothing to do with me," or "If I didn't feel bad, what would keep me from doing something like that again?"

Often, it was clear to us that what had occurred was an accident, that our clients had done their best in an impossible situation, that there was no way they could have prevented what happened, that there was no possible good outcome or way to "save the day," or that our client had reacted out of fear or pain under unimaginably difficult circumstances. Yet, as therapists, we could not just lay this on the table. If we were to say "You did the best you could" or "It wasn't your fault" our clients would not feel relief; rather they would feel like we did not understand the situation, like we did not understand them. With a client population already at high risk of drop out, such a blunt approach could be the end of their willingness to let us help them. We understood that beliefs about their role in the trauma and emotional pain resulting from the trauma ran too deep for a pat statement from us. We realized we needed a more targeted approach to help people make sense of, and recover from, their trauma-related guilt and shame and sometimes moral injury. We looked at the literature and our clinical experiences to come up with an integrated model as to why these beliefs about what one did or did not do caused so much pain and dysfunction, so fundamentally changed how people saw themselves, and were so difficult to shift. From here, the Nonadaptive Guilt and Shame (NAGS) model was born (see Chapter 2), and we started developing TrIGR in 2008 to give therapists tools to help their clients recover from such debilitating posttraumatic and moral injury-related guilt and shame.

As we began to offer TrIGR to our clients and study TrIGR through research, interest in guilt and shame in the broader field of trauma was also growing. In 2013, an updated version of the Diagnostic and Statistical Manual (DSM5; American Psychiatric Association, 2013) was published and for the first time contained a symptom for PTSD that included guilt and shame. Interest in moral injury began to grow (Frankfurt & Frazier, 2016; Jinkerson, 2016; Litz et al., 2009). Mental health researchers began to pay more attention to the role of guilt and shame in posttraumatic distress. Clinicians from across the United States and abroad began to contact us to learn about TrIGR.

Over the past decade we have continued to study TrIGR, use it with our clients, share it with our colleagues, and modify it as we learned more. This book is the culmination of our work with hundreds of clients, feedback from other clinicians who have used TrIGR with their own clients, and our own and others' research. We are thankful for the opportunity to share TrIGR with you and hope you find the intervention helpful with your clients.

Overview of this book

We begin by presenting background information on the connection between trauma-related guilt and shame, moral injury, and common co-occurring mental health problems such as PTSD, depression, or substance use (Chapter 2). We then introduce TrIGR (Chapter 3) and walk readers through the process of deciding if TrIGR is an appropriate treatment strategy (Chapter 4), conducting assessments (Chapter 5), and preparing clients to engage in the treatment (Chapter 6). We included a chapter on therapist self-care (Chapter 8) because while helping clients heal from trauma is incredibly rewarding, it can also be very difficult. Thus, we offer information on signs of burnout and some strategies for self-care to prevent burnout and return from it if it occurs. We also included a chapter on considerations for specific client groups, like military Veterans who have experienced moral injury and survivors of sexual assault (Chapter 7) and a chapter on delivering TrIGR in group (Chapter 9). The final part of the book is the TrIGR therapist manual, which includes sample scripts and case examples to illustrate and highlight key aspects of the therapy, and the client workbook.

CHAPTER 2

The connection between guilt and shame and mental health problems

In this chapter, we explore the concepts of guilt and shame from trauma and moral injury and talk about how they relate to common mental health problems. We then present our model of why people suffer from guilt and shame related to trauma and moral injury to set the stage for the next chapter (Chapter 3) where we explain how Trauma Informed Guilt Reduction (TrIGR) therapy helps to resolve this suffering.

Defining trauma-related guilt and shame

The terms "guilt" and "shame" have been used in many different ways in mental health fields and in our general vernacular. Guilt and shame are often considered "self-conscious" secondary emotions. Unlike primary emotions like happiness, sadness, or anger which are viewed as biologically driven emotional states triggered in a reflexive manner in response to environmental cues (Kim, Thibodeau, & Jorgensen, 2011), secondary emotions arise from complex thoughts (Tangey & Dearing, 2002). In other words, trauma-related guilt and shame consist of a feeling or emotional component as well as a thinking/cognitive component (Kubany & Watson, 2003). Consistent with this conceptualization, guilt and shame have been defined as distressing emotions arising from negatively appraising a situation or oneself in comparison to valued standards (Lewis, 1971; Tangey & Dearing, 2002). An example of such an appraisal may be "People should take care of their loved ones, so I failed my loved one when I didn't stop her suicide."

In TrIGR and throughout this book, we talk a great deal about guilt and shame so it is important for us to clarify how the two differ from each other. In her seminal theory, Lewis (1971) proposed the difference between guilt and shame comes down to the focus of one's self-evaluation. With guilt, the focus is on one's *behavior* ("I've done something bad"). With shame, the

Trauma Informed Guilt Reduction Therapy
https://doi.org/10.1016/B978-0-12-814780-1.00002-2

focus is on the *entire self* ("I am a bad person"). The construct of shame is often further divided into negative self-evaluation ("I can't believe I am someone who would do that") and concern about evaluation by others ("What would my wife think if she knew this about me?") (Gilbert & Andrews, 1998).

Not all guilt is considered to be problematic. Social psychology suggests that guilt related to common every day experiences can be adaptive (Tangey & Dearing, 2002). For example, feeling guilt about forgetting to feed a pet before leaving for work may inspire someone to post reminders on their refrigerator or to wake up earlier so as not to be so rushed in the morning.

Guilt and shame related to traumatic events

Guilt and shame are very common among trauma survivors. People who have experienced certain types of traumatic events, such as interpersonal violence (Scheffer Lindgren & Renck, 2008), sexual trauma (Michalopoulos et al., 2015), and combat (Farnsworth, Drescher, Nieuwsma, Walser, & Currier, 2014), are especially likely to experience guilt and shame. However, survivors of any type of trauma can experience guilt and shame and there is research showing that survivors of motor vehicle accidents (Amstadter & Vernon, 2008), natural and man-made disasters (Carmassi et al., 2017), those who have experienced the traumatic loss of a loved one (Pitman, Osborn, Rantell, & King, 2016), and refugees impacted by war (Stotz, Elbert, Müller, & Schauer, 2015), can all experience guilt related to the trauma.

Guilt and shame related to interpersonal violence

Survivors of interpersonal violence often express self-blame for not having left the first time the partner became abusive and, for those who had children, exposing them to the abuse. Survivors also report feeling guilty for the abuse itself, often concluding that they must have done something to deserve it. Child abuse similarly often engenders self-blame and shame (Messman-Moore & Coates, 2007). Abuse survivors were often implicitly or explicitly blamed for the abuse and put down by the abuser (Carlson, Furby, Armstrong, & Shlaes, 1997), and sometimes by others too (Finkelhor, 1987; Herman, 1992), and it is not uncommon for them to internalize this blame. Victims may also place blame upon themselves rather than on the perpetrator as a way to maintain an attachment to a perpetrator that they depend on financially or emotionally (e.g., "If I were a better person, I wouldn't make him so mad").

Shame is common among survivors of sexual abuse, who often view themselves as "damaged goods," and who are more likely to be blamed than other trauma survivors (Amstadter & Vernon, 2008). Shame is also common if the abuse involved a social taboo such as incest, or if the survivor became sexually aroused or experienced any pleasant emotions during the assault, which is quite common because of automatic physiological responses over which the survivor had no control (see Romano & De Luca, 2001).

Military veterans and moral injury

Military service members and Veterans are at particular risk of experiencing trauma-related guilt and shame (Jinkerson, 2016; Litz et al., 2009). This is not surprising given that combat and war often call for behaviors that may not be in line with one's values outside of the context of war. War Veterans may have witnessed or participated in massacres and atrocities. They may have killed civilians, including children. They may have found that they felt nothing or felt pleasure in the moment they killed someone and now struggle with what that means about them.

Wartime trauma where one participates in, or witnesses, acts that violate deeply held morals or values has been termed moral injury (Litz et al., 2009). A predominant characteristic of moral injury is a reaction of guilt and shame. In fact, a recent review defined moral injury as follows: "The moral injury syndrome was proposed to describe the constellation of shame and guilt-based disturbances that some combat Veterans experience after engaging in wartime acts of commission (e.g., killing) or omission (e.g., failing to prevent atrocities)"(Frankfurt & Frazier, 2016; Litz et al., 2009). Another review defined moral injury in the following way: "Moral injury is a particular type of psychological trauma characterized by intense guilt, shame…" (Jinkerson, 2016). Moral injury is also associated with self-injurious behaviors such as substance use and suicidality and self-handicapping behaviors such as not taking part in activities that would facilitate recovery (Frankfurt & Frazier, 2016). These behaviors may be driven by guilt and shame beliefs stemming from the moral injury, such as "I do not deserve to do well in life or feel better because of what I did." Spiritual conflict and loss of trust are other common characteristics of moral injury (Litz et al., 2009). Anyone who experiences a traumatic event that violates deeply held morals and values may experience moral injury. Moral injury is not limited only to Veterans or wartime traumas.

Why do some people feel guilt and shame after trauma?

Social psychologists have explained the function of guilt and shame in the following ways: guilt and shame are rooted in prosocial adaptation (Tangey & Dearing, 2002), that is, these emotions urge us to behave in ways that increase our survival within a social context. For example, if we have done something to upset someone, feeling guilty may compel us to do something to repair the relationship such as apologize, make amends, or avoid doing the same thing in the future. Feeling shame induces submissive behaviors such as slouching or averted eyes that can help pacify someone we might have angered or threatened through our actions. So according to social psychology, these guilt- and shame-related behaviors help us maintain relationships and avoid being ousted from groups we depend on.

Guilt and shame may be adaptive responses immediately after a trauma because they prompt survivors to evaluate what happened and their role in it and to try to repair the situation if needed. Evaluating what happened also allows survivors to consider if and how they might want to behave differently in the future. However, clients who experience distress following a traumatic event often avoid trauma memories and associated thoughts and feelings, thereby limiting the possibility of processing guilt in this adaptive way. Unfortunately, avoidant coping, or the tendency to avoid trauma reminders and thoughts/feelings, is very common among people who go on to develop mental health problems such as PTSD following trauma. Avoidance can be a reason why trauma survivors do not reflect on why they feel guilt, which can leave the feelings of guilt lingering long term and allow them to evolve into shame as well.

Among clients who do appraise why the trauma happened, posttraumatic appraisals are not 100% accurate and may also contribute to the development of posttraumatic guilt and/or shame. For example, a strong pre-trauma belief in a "just world," the idea that people get what they deserve, can lead someone to believe that the trauma they experienced was their fault or deserved (Lerner & Montada, 1998). It is understandable that someone might want to hold on to this belief because it can provide a sense of control and predictability over what happens (Breitenbecher, 2006). However, it is not an accurate belief. Many (good and bad) things happen to people regardless of whether they deserve them.

Another pre-trauma belief that often leads to trauma-related guilt and shame is that of responsibility. Leaders or supervisors are often trained to believe that they are responsible for anything caused by or that happens to their subordinates. Then, when people get hurt, leaders may blame themselves and believe the injuries were their fault, even if they had no actual control in the situation. This is a common practice in the military (Doty & Doty, 2012). Indeed, we have often treated military unit commanders suffering from trauma-related guilt and shame because of the injury or death of one or more individuals in their unit.

The impact of trauma-related guilt and shame on mental health

People who experience guilt and shame following trauma are more likely to develop and have more severe mental health problems such as PTSD (Gaudet, Sowers, Nugent, & Boriskin, 2016; Pugh, Taylor, & Berry, 2015; Saraiya & Lopez-Castro, 2016), depression (Browne, Trim, Myers, & Norman, 2015; Marx et al., 2010), and substance use (Wilkins, Myers, Goldsmith, Buzzella, & Norman, 2013) than those who do not. Guilt and shame are also associated with greater likelihood of experiencing suicidal ideation and suicide attempts (Bryan et al., 2013a, 2013b; Tripp & McDevitt-Murphy, 2017) and having more severe impairment in social and occupational functioning (Norman et al., 2018) than trauma survivors who do not experience guilt and shame.

Putting it all together: The NAGS model

Our clinical work and the research we summarized here led us to believe there was a need for a psychotherapy that would specifically help clients whose primary suffering was from guilt, shame, and moral injury from trauma. Once we decided to develop this therapy, our first step was to come up with a model to explain the relationships among trauma, guilt, and shame, and the problems and symptoms we were seeing in our clients. We would then use this model to develop the therapy. Our model, the Nonadaptive Guilt and Shame (NAGS) model, is summarized in Fig. 1 and explained below.

The NAGS model starts by considering what happens right after a traumatic event. When someone experiences a trauma, they may or may not feel guilt. If they do feel guilt, they may or may not reflect on why they are experiencing this distressing emotion. Examined guilt has the potential to serve a prosocial function in that it may encourage someone to try to repair a relationship that was hurt or to change behavior to be more in

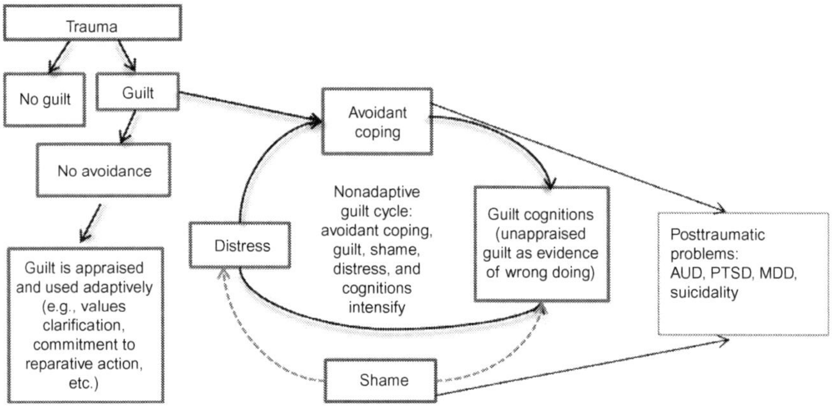

Fig. 1 Nonadaptive Guilt and Shame (NAGS) model.

line with values. However, clients who experience distress following a traumatic event often avoid trauma memories and associated thoughts and feelings, thereby limiting the possibility of processing guilt in this adaptive way. They may also come to inaccurate conclusions about their role in the trauma ("If I behaved better, she would not have hit me") that can contribute to guilt and shame. People who do not examine their guilt because of avoidant coping and/or who come to faulty conclusions may develop nonadaptive guilt where the feeling of guilt is taken as evidence of wrong doing ("I feel bad, so I must have done something bad"). Believing "I did something bad" can lead to feeling even worse, which creates a cycle of negatively spiraling thoughts and feelings that increase the sense of guilt. When the guilt thought of "I did something bad" generalizes to the self ("I am bad"), we see shame develop. In almost all cases, our clients come to us feeling both guilt and shame. It is not unusual for clients to present with long held beliefs such as, "I don't deserve to be loved" or "I deserve to suffer." This escalating spiral of non-adaptive guilt and shame is the heart of the NAGS model. We help clients identify their non-adaptive guilt and shame cognitions in Modules 1 and 2 of TrIGR and help them reexamine nonadaptive thoughts in Module 2.

We then considered why NAGS is associated with more severe mental health problems (PTSD, depression), more problem behaviors like substance use, more suicidality, and more severe functioning problems than among trauma survivors who do not feel guilt. First, guilt and shame can intensify mental health and functioning problems after trauma because of beliefs such as "I don't deserve to feel better because of what I did," which may perpetuate problem behaviors such as alcohol/substance use and get in the way of benefiting from treatment. We see this in clients who come to treatment with a great deal of ambivalence about getting better. They may express their ambivalence by not completing homework or by dropping out of treatment. This kind of ambivalence is so common in trauma survivors who experience guilt and shame that we have a chapter in this book on how to address it (Chapter 6, Preparing Your Clients for TrIGR).

Indeed, research has found that greater trauma-related guilt and shame predict more avoidance, which in turn predicts more severe posttraumatic distress (Held, Owens, & Anderson, 2015; Street & Arias, 2001). For many clients, this cycle has been in place for years by the time they come to us. After a while, avoidance and distress significantly limit functioning so that for many of our clients, meeting career or educational goals, engaging in meaningful activities, or having satisfying personal relationships becomes nearly impossible. For these reasons, helping our clients improve social and occupational functioning (which we focus on in Module 3 of TrIGR) is just as important as helping reduce their trauma-related symptoms.

Another way that NAGS contributes to the severity of mental health problems and functioning is that avoidance interferes with the ability to make values-based decisions. For example, among combatants, experiencing rage and hostility can serve as a way to escape fear, guilt, shame, and other distress associated with moral injury, but paradoxically can contribute to aggression and violence, which can lead to more guilt and shame (see Itzhaky, Avidor, & Solomon, 2017). Similarly, a parent avoiding feeling guilty about not feeling connected to their child may be less likely to spend more time with their child because doing so brings up the feelings of guilt and shame. In Module 3, we focus on helping clients reconnect with values and set goals to live in line with values.

NAGS often stems from moral injury. In fact, NAGS offers a framework for why moral injury is associated with guilt and shame as well as self-injurious and self-sabotaging behaviors. Guilt and shame result from having violated deeply held morals and values during the trauma. Ironically, the guilt and shame beliefs and associated distress continue to keep trauma survivors from living in line with values in the present. Rather, those with moral injury make take part in self-injurious behaviors such as substance use or self-sabotaging behaviors such as dropping out of treatment because of beliefs that they do not deserve better.

CHAPTER 3

Overview of TrIGR

Using the Nonadaptive Guilt and Shame (NAGS) model as a framework, we designed Trauma Informed Guilt Reduction (TrIGR) therapy to reduce posttraumatic distress tied to guilt, shame, and moral injury. TrIGR therapy is a brief (3-module) manualized intervention that utilizes some of the strategies developed and tested by Kubany and colleagues (Kubany et al., 1995; Kubany & Watson, 2003), as well as additional approaches to address guilt and shame. TrIGR also includes some of the values identification and commitment work formalized in acceptance and commitment therapy (ACT; Hayes, Strosahl, & Wilson, 2016). In TrIGR, trauma survivors are taught to more accurately appraise their guilt and shame cognitions and reidentify and reengage in their values as a part of their recovery from posttraumatic distress and moral injury.

Kubany and colleagues identified four common cognitive errors among people who experience trauma-related guilt and suggested that reappraising such beliefs would lead to reductions in guilt and related distress (Kubany, 1994; Kubany & Ralston, 1998). These cognitive errors are hindsight bias (believing that the outcome was known at the time of the trauma), lack of justification (believing there was no or little justification for the course of action one chose to take), responsibility (believing one was solely or mostly responsible for the traumatic event), and wrongdoing (believing one purposely did something that was wrong or violated important values).

Additionally, we found that clients, regardless of the type of trauma they had experienced, were wary of letting go of guilt. In some cases, this was because self-blame and shame helped them survive the trauma by giving them a way to maintain a relationship with someone they depended on who was hurting them. Among those who experienced a traumatic loss,

Trauma Informed Guilt Reduction Therapy
https://doi.org/10.1016/B978-0-12-814780-1.00003-4

holding on to guilt was sometimes a way to honor a memory. Sometimes, feeling guilt gave someone a way to maintain a sense of control ("The accident happened because I did something wrong, not because the world is completely uncontrollable"). In many cases, our clients believed that holding onto the guilt was a way to live in line with their values ("If I didn't feel guilty about what I did, what would stop me from doing it again?"). As per our NAGS model, taking steps to live in line with values can help clients honor their values in more functional ways than suffering from guilt and shame, which in turn can reduce guilt-related distress. For these reasons, TrIGR also includes a focus on identifying personal values and setting a plan to live in line with values in a meaningful, positive way going forward (Orsillo & Batten, 2005).

TrIGR consists of three modules: (1) psychoeducation regarding the role of guilt and shame in posttraumatic distress and common types of trauma-related guilt and shame; (2) appraisal of common thinking errors, and helping the client recall the fuller, more accurate context of what occurred during the time of the trauma; and (3) helping clients identify important values and collaboratively developing a plan that allows the client to live in line with these values going forward. The therapy can be administered during four to seven 60–90-min sessions.

Module 1 is split into two sessions 1 and 2. Session 1 introduces the NAGS model and why guilt and shame can be the cause of so much pain and dysfunction. We highlight that guilt can be adaptive, but when unexamined, distressful feelings of guilt can be taken as evidence of wrongdoing ("I feel bad, so I must have done something wrong"), which can create and perpetuate a cycle of feeling increasingly worse and more certain of wrongdoing as time goes by. Session 2 reviews common posttraumatic reactions such as symptoms of PTSD, depression, and substance use. The "fight, flight, or freeze" reaction to traumatic events is reviewed as we have found that trauma survivors frequently blame themselves for responding during trauma in a way that may have been physiologically beyond their control ("It was my fault because I froze").

We then review information that shows that guilt is common following trauma and review common sources of trauma-related guilt (Kubany, 1994; Opp & Samson, 1989). Within the therapist manual, we provide examples of common sources of guilt across trauma types including Veterans with military trauma, first responders, sexual assault survivors, and loved ones of suicide completers. Review of these common sources of guilt includes discussion about which types of guilt the client experiences and psychoeducation about why people may have reacted in these ways. For example, if clients feel ashamed because they felt pleasure while being sexually assaulted, the therapist describes how it is normal and involuntary to respond physiologically, even when being assaulted. Lastly, a key component of this session is to start to identify clients' beliefs about their trauma to assist with moving into the appraisal skills of Module 2.

Module 2 uses cognitive restructuring techniques grounded in cognitive behavioral therapy (CBT) developed by Kubany (Kubany & Manke, 1995) to help clients evaluate the four types of cognitive errors contributing to trauma-related guilt identified in the previous research (Kubany et al., 2004). To identify cognitions that are associated with guilt (e.g., "I should have…" or "I shouldn't have…"), the therapist conducts a fairly detailed review of the traumatic event with the client at the beginning of the session. This detailed review is needed because what may initially appear to be the source of guilt ("I killed someone during the battle") may in fact turn out to be a far more nuanced cognition upon further exploration ("I was justified in killing the insurgent, but I shouldn't have enjoyed it"). Each of the four cognitive errors is reviewed; however, the amount of time dedicated to each error is tailored to the client's needs and experiences. Examples are used to illustrate each concept and then the concept is discussed in relation to the client's traumatic event. For example, a source of guilt related to moral injury may be shooting someone in combat who looked as if they may be a threat but later turned out to be unarmed. In reviewing hindsight bias, the client may express beliefs that "I knew he wasn't a threat, but I shot anyway." The therapist leads the client through several exercises to normalize how common it is to come to believe, after the fact, that someone had information they did not actually have until later. Therapists then explore with clients what they actually knew at the time of the trauma vs what they came to believe they knew after the fact given the negative outcome. Clients are given the opportunity to come to a different conclusion such as "I wish I had known they were unarmed, but I didn't know one way or the other."

In the justification analysis, the therapist and the client explore what choices were truly available at the time of the trauma as people frequently believe, after the fact, that there must have been a way for a better outcome. Clients write down all of the options available to them during the event, such as fighting back, running away, yelling, distracting, and numbing oneself until the sexual assault is over, and the potential pros and cons of each. This is often helpful when someone has been focusing on the perceived positive outcome of an alternative choice without consideration of the possible negative consequences of that choice, or similarly, when focused on the negative outcome of the choice that was made without consideration of the positive aspects of that choice such as "I was not as strong as my assailant, and if I had tried to run, fight back, or yell, that probably would have made them mad and hurt me more or even kill me." This examination generally leads to the realization that there were no "good" options, that all options would have led to some undesirable outcome, that an idealized positive option they may think of now did not exist at the time, or that the option taken by the client was either the best of the available options in some way or no worse than the other available options.

In the responsibility analysis, clients initially rate the percent that they believe they are responsible for what happened on a scale from 0% to 100%. The therapist then leads the client through an exercise to demonstrate that there are multiple factors that contributed to the outcome. For example, the therapist may flick the light switch and ask why the lights went on and off to which the client generally responds, "because you flicked the switch." The therapist agrees and then points out additional contributing factors such as a properly electrically wired building, a working light bulb, and the invention of electricity also contributed to the lights going on and off. The client and the therapist then brainstorm together to identify all of the other factors that contributed to the client's traumatic event and the percent to which the client feels each was responsible for what happened. For example, contributing factors for a woman staying with an abusive partner include cultural or religious beliefs that marriage is forever, not having resources to leave, not wanting to leave the kids with her abusive partner but not having legal recourse to take them with her, learned helplessness, etc. Clients are then able to view their self-assigned level of responsibility (which is typically 90% or above) relative to the total of these other factors and rerate their level of responsibility as a much lower percentage. Therapists are instructed never try to talk to clients out of a sense of responsibility (e.g., to say things like "You were just doing your job" or "It wasn't your fault") as these statements can feel alienating and inauthentic. Rather, therapists help their clients take the full context in which the traumatic event occurred into account.

Finally, in the wrongdoing analysis, the difference between intentionally setting out to do harm and an unfolding bad outcome are discussed.

An illustrative example might be breaking a glass by knocking it off a table by accident versus throwing a glass against a wall with the intent to break it. This discussion is generally straightforward for many clients where the clients can acknowledge that they did not intend to cause harm, for example, choosing to go a shorter way because of traffic and getting into a car accident. However, this discussion may be more complicated with some clients. For example, a Veteran whose moral injury is due to having hurt or killed others outside of the rules of engagement may have gone back to a village sometime after a battle and killed additional people in order to seek revenge for the death of a comrade. In such cases, helping the client consider the context of war, emotions that were at play such as intense anger and grief, the extent of the Veteran's guilt/remorse and how much he or she has suffered since the event, or if the client ever intends to do anything similar in the future can help give some context to the concept of wrongdoing.

Within the wrongdoing analysis, clients also identify what values they were living by during the time of the trauma, and learn that they may have had values that were conflicting with one another. Wrongdoing also shows up as a cognitive error in child abuse survivors who came to believe that they must have deserved the abuse. Believing this allowed them to maintain attachment to their abusive caregiver and therefore increased their chance of survival. As a reminder, the goal is not to try to lead the client to believe that the trauma "was not his/her fault" but rather to help clients put the traumatic event and their actions and choices into context to help them move toward a life marked by less suffering and impairment.

Module 2 can be repeated for clients who have more than one source of trauma-related guilt and shame. Module 2 ends with a discussion of the purpose that guilt and shame have served in the client's life and what it might mean to feel less of these. This discussion often reveals beliefs about the function of the guilt or shame and reasons the client may be hesitant to let go of them. For example, clients have reported to us that feeling guilt and/or shame helps them honor the individuals who died or were injured in the trauma, or that they do not deserve to feel happy because of what they did or because they did not deserve to live or remain unscathed any more than the person(s) who died or were injured. Identifying the function of guilt is critical to help the client identify alternative ways to express emotions and live according to the values that underlie this function.

Discussing the function of guilt at the end of Module 2 allows the therapist and client to transition to Module 3 where the focus is on identifying the client's values and ways to live a value-driven life. Clients who feel guilt, shame, and moral injury from trauma often believe that they may be amoral or that morals and values do not matter to them, whereas the fact that they have suffered so deeply because they violated a value actually suggests that values and morals are very important to them. The therapist guides the client to identify values in domains that are important to the client such as family, work, and spirituality, set long- and short-term goals consistent with these values, and troubleshoot how to overcome potential obstacles. Some clients want to take reparative action. That is, they want to do something to make up for the harm they caused or to honor/remember someone who died during the trauma. If a client expresses a strong desire to take reparative action for their role in the trauma (e.g., doing something for family members of someone who was killed during a car crash or starting a fund for someone who died in combat), the therapist helps the client make a realistic plan to do so in a way that minimizes the likelihood of possibly distressing others and helps set realistic expectations for the outcome. For example, the therapist can help make sure clients are aware that they cannot control the outcome of their plan even with the best intentions.

The therapy ends with a plan of specific actions the client can take to continue to work toward a value-driven life. The therapist and the client also plan for how to continue on a path of recovery and how to recognize if more help is needed in the future.

PART 2

Preparation and case related considerations

PART 2 PREPARATION AND CASE RELATED CONSIDERATIONS

CHAPTER 4

Is TrIGR the right choice for your client?

In this chapter, we consider which clients may be good candidates for Trauma Informed Guilt Reduction (TrIGR) therapy and when to offer TrIGR relative to other treatments such as those that are for specific diagnoses such as PTSD or depression.

Signs that TrIGR may be a good option for your client

TrIGR is ideal for a client who reports having experienced one or more traumatic events, feels guilt and/or shame related to the trauma, and suffers distress and functional impairment because of the trauma. TrIGR is also appropriate for military and Veteran clients who experience guilt and shame stemming from moral injury. The word *trauma* is used in many ways in the English language. In TrIGR, we conceptualize trauma as a life-threatening event, one where a person thought they or someone else might die, or witnessed actual death. We also include sexual assault, even in cases when the threat of death was not present. This conceptualization of trauma is consistent with DSM-5 (American Psychiatric Association, 2013) and the International Classification of Disease, 10th Edition (ICD-10; World Health Organization, 1992). In Chapter 5, we provide specific recommendations for how to assess whether your client experienced this kind of trauma. Clients with tell-tale signs of Nonadaptive Guilt and Shame (NAGS) have persistent, intrusive, unwanted thoughts and ruminations about something they think they should or should not have done during the trauma, or about their sense of "badness" or of deserving bad things. Clients who present with a trauma history, NAGS in relation to one or more traumas, and functional impairment may benefit from focusing on guilt and shame in treatment.

Trauma Informed Guilt Reduction Therapy
https://doi.org/10.1016/B978-0-12-814780-1.00004-6

Signs that TrIGR is not a good choice

A client who does not feel guilt, regret, or shame about the trauma is generally not a good candidate for TrIGR. This lack of NAGS may be because a client is at peace with their actions during a trauma or, in rare cases, because they may have personality features where they do not experience remorse (e.g., antisocial personality disorder). Sometimes it is hard to tell if a client truly does not experience guilt or shame, or if the client is so expert at avoiding these feelings that they are hard for the therapist to identify. The assessment strategies in Chapter 5 will help you to decide if your client is a good candidate for TrIGR.

We have from time to time received referrals of clients to TrIGR from clinicians who assumed a client had NAGS based on the kind of trauma they experienced (e.g., they had taken a life in combat or kept children in an abusive home). Through thorough assessment we sometimes found that while these clients may have PTSD or other problems stemming from these traumas, they did not suffer from guilt or shame. Based on these experiences, we urge therapists to assess guilt and shame specifically to ensure TrIGR is an appropriate treatment choice.

In most circumstances, TrIGR would not be recommended if a client does not remember the trauma. It is very common for trauma survivors to forget some parts of the trauma, but if they have almost no memory of it at all, it will not be feasible to do the trauma debriefing portion of TrIGR. Like other trauma-focused psychotherapies, TrIGR would not be appropriate for clients who have severe forms of cognitive impairment, active psychosis or mania, or other symptoms or behaviors that make it difficult for them to track what the therapist is saying and engage with external reality. We have, however, treated clients with well-managed psychotic disorders and ones with mild and moderate traumatic brain injury. Similarly, TrIGR is not a good first-line treatment for clients who are in acute danger of harming themselves or others, or who otherwise have serious limitations in impulse control. When safety issues such as risk of harming oneself or others are present, those should always be addressed first. Therapists are advised to follow good clinical practice, to address acute safety and therapy interfering behaviors prior to beginning TrIGR, and to continue adjunctive strategies to maintain safety and stabilization throughout the course of treatment as needed.

However, we do not recommend waiting to start trauma-focused treatment such as TrIGR until all treatment-interfering behaviors are completely eliminated because the trauma may actually be driving some of these behaviors. Alcohol and drug abuse are perfect examples. Substance abuse is common among people who have experienced trauma. Reducing NAGS and other trauma-related distress may be critical to help clients reduce substance use, especially if they are using alcohol or drugs to cope with their trauma-related symptoms. A trauma-focused treatment such as TrIGR, together with substance use treatment, may be critical to a client's recovery. We offer suggestions for how to address treatment-interfering behaviors, including substance abuse, during TrIGR in Chapters 6 and 7 and in the Therapist Manual.

Similarly, avoidance is not a disqualifier for TrIGR as it is almost universal among people who experience posttraumatic distress; however, a client must be willing to talk about their trauma to a certain extent, discuss feelings of guilt and shame, and experience emotions that may come up during therapy. Sometimes even assessment of whether guilt and shame are present may be difficult for clients. Trauma survivors who are dealing with posttraumatic distress engage in avoidance in many different ways, some of which can evade accurate assessment because they include behaviors that at first glance appear to be the opposite of avoidance. For example, some clients may avoid by hyperfocusing on some other aspect(s) of the trauma or another trauma-related emotion like anger, or discussing another distressing trauma that is not eliciting guilt and shame. Clients who are stuck in a NAGS cycle can alternate between intrusive thoughts about the trauma and avoiding thinking about the trauma. Some clients can become so good at avoiding that they may report very few or no intrusive symptoms. Because of avoidance, and because of deep feelings of shame, many clients do not readily disclose trauma histories or trauma-related guilt and shame. Ways to facilitate clients' disclosure and strategies for helping clients decide if they are ready for TrIGR are discussed in Chapters 6 and 7 and in the therapist manual.

TrIGR can be appropriate for clients who intentionally caused harm during the trauma, as long as guilt and/or shame are present. For example, we have worked with Veterans who in a moment of deep hurt and anguish during combat killed someone they were not required to kill. Now they live with debilitating guilt and shame every day. In such a situation, TrIGR likely would be appropriate. On the other hand, if someone has no remorse, guilt, or shame, TrIGR would not be appropriate. Again, the goal of TrIGR is never to convince someone that the trauma was "not their fault," but rather to help clients put their role in the traumatic event into context to find a way to move forward with less suffering and impairment. Additionally, recall that being stuck in the NAGS cycle means that an individual has less access to their values, is less likely to engage in value-driven behavior, and therefore is more likely to engage in behaviors that lead to feeling more guilt and shame. We developed TrIGR to interrupt this cycle and help clients reacquaint themselves with their values and commit to value-driven behavior.

TrIGR can be modified to accommodate clients with reading difficulties, non-English speakers, or those with some cognitive deficits. For example, therapists can create simplified versions of written worksheets. Simplified worksheets have been used with clients with traumatic brain injury-related cognitive deficits and with illiterate non-English speakers in the Congo, with good outcomes for Cognitive Processing Therapy (CPT) (Bass et al., 2013; Chard, Schumm, McIlvain, Bailey, & Parkinson, 2011). Additionally, TrIGR sessions are audio recorded and clients listen to the recordings for homework. This allows clients to learn and practice skills verbally.

When is the best time for a client to complete TrIGR?

NAGS may be accompanied by PTSD, mood and anxiety disorders, substance use, anger and aggression, and/or suicidal/self-injurious behaviors. All of these problems disrupt and cause impairment in functioning in a number of life areas such as with friends, with family, and at work. We are often asked when to offer TrIGR relative to other psychotherapies that address these problems. For example, if a client has PTSD would we offer TrIGR before or after an evidence-based PTSD treatment such as CPT, prolonged exposure (PE), or eye movement desensitization and reprocessing (EMDR)? The answer to this question is, "It depends." As of yet, we do not have research to guide this decision. However, it is clear that there is no one path that fits every client. In our own work, we have offered TrIGR as a first-line treatment and we have done TrIGR with clients who had already completed treatment for PTSD, depression, or other problems but were still suffering from guilt and shame. We have seen clients benefit from TrIGR in both these circumstances.

Because PE, CPT, and EMDR have been studied for many years and work well with clients who have experienced all kinds of traumas, one of these treatments may be a good starting point. However, if a client wants a briefer treatment, does not have PTSD, or wants to work specifically on guilt and shame, TrIGR may be a good place to start. It is also common for clients to complete an evidence-based PTSD treatment and still have some residual symptoms (e.g., Karlin & Cross, 2014). Guilt and shame are problems that may persist after PTSD treatment (Larsen, Fleming, & Resick, 2018; Owens, Chard, & Ann Cox, 2008). Not all clients will have PTSD or any disorder, while others will have several disorders. TrIGR can be a good option in such cases because it is a transdiagnostic intervention. It can also be a good choice for clients who do not want to commit to a longer treatment as it can be completed in 4–7 sessions. We often offer TrIGR to clients who have completed other treatments but still suffer from guilt and shame related to their trauma and many times we have seen TrIGR take these clients to the next level of their recovery.

We generally do not recommend delivering TrIGR at the same time as other trauma-focused psychotherapies because each of these asks clients to immerse themselves in the treatment model and also often each requires a sizable time commitment (i.e., coming to therapy, completing daily homework assignments). For these reasons, doing TrIGR and another trauma-focused or manualized treatment at the same time may be confusing to clients and also dilute the effects of the treatments.

We do, however, recommend treating other comorbidities such as substance abuse or insomnia, at the same time as TrIGR. This is consistent with various treatment guidelines (e.g., VA/DOD Clinical Practice Guidelines; Department of Veterans Affairs & Department of Defense, 2017) that recommend that evidence-based treatments for common comorbidities should be offered at the same time as trauma-focused treatment.

One method we recommend for deciding when to offer TrIGR is shared decision-making (Elwyn et al., 2012). Client choice is a positive predictor of clients initiating psychotherapy (Dwight-Johnson, Unutzer, Sherbourne, Tang, & Wells, 2001), staying in therapy longer (Rokke, Tomhave, & Jocic, 1999), and, in some studies, of successfully completing psychotherapy (Laugharne & Priebe, 2006). In shared decision-making, you and your client use the best available evidence and client preference to make decisions together. In this approach, the therapist first lets the client know that treatment options exist. The therapist then describes the treatment options in detail, including an overview of the treatment and the underlying treatment model, the time commitment involved for attending sessions and homework, and the research evidence behind the treatment (i.e., how well the treatment works and for whom). The final step is helping the client make a decision that takes into account the information about the treatments as well as the client's goals for treatment. This collaborative approach can help guide if and when to offer TrIGR.

We suggest these same guidelines for when to offer TrIGR to clients with moral injury (Norman, Wilkins, Myers, & Allard, 2014). TrIGR is designed to address guilt and shame stemming from moral injury as well as associated self-injurious and self-handicapping behaviors. If PTSD is present, an evidence-based treatment such as PE, CPT, or EMDR may be a good starting point. However, for clients who do not have PTSD, who prefer to focus on guilt and shame exclusively, or who continue to have moral injury-related guilt and shame following other treatments, TrIGR can be a good option. TrIGR is not designed to address spiritual conflict or loss of trust that sometimes accompany moral injury so other intervention, and possible collaboration with a chaplain or religious/spiritual advisor may be helpful.

CHAPTER 5

Assessment of guilt, shame, PTSD, and other posttraumatic distress

In this chapter, we discuss why assessing guilt, shame, and commonly related symptoms and problems is important prior to beginning Trauma Informed Guilt Reduction (TrIGR) therapy and throughout the treatment. We then give examples of validated measures that can help you assess if TrIGR is right for your client and if your client is benefitting from TrIGR.

Assessment plays a critical role in TrIGR. Assessment prior to treatment helps determine the client's problems and inform the treatment plan. Assessment during treatment helps you to understand if clients are benefiting from the intervention and what other needs they may have. For these reasons, we recommend assessment as part of the intake/treatment planning process prior to beginning TrIGR and using a short assessment battery of measures at the beginning of every other session during the therapy. Specifically, assessing for posttraumatic guilt and shame helps to determine if TrIGR is a good fit for the client. Assessing for moral injury, common forms of posttraumatic distress and for safety concerns, such as risk of suicide, further informs case conceptualization and treatment planning, and helps identify any specific issues that may need to be addressed during or prior to engaging in TrIGR. We also recommend assessing functioning and quality of life to help you understand how treatment may be impacting your clients' day to day lives. Structured diagnostic interviews and validated self-report measures provide additional information to what we typically capture in an unstructured clinical interview in a relatively brief amount of time and make it easier to detect change over time.

Using a structured clinician administered interview to assess for current and/or lifetime psychiatric diagnoses and to understand symptom severity will help to determine if TrIGR is an appropriate intervention for your client.

Trauma Informed Guilt Reduction Therapy
https://doi.org/10.1016/B978-0-12-814780-1.00005-8

It can also help inform if a client may require a higher level of care such as inpatient or residential treatment for issues such as suicidal risk, active manic symptoms, or severe eating disorder symptoms, whether they may benefit from concurrent treatment for a comorbidity such as insomnia or substance use, and/or require ongoing monitoring during the course of treatment for issues such as alcohol use (Persons, 2012). A thorough initial assessment of psychiatric diagnoses and symptom severity also facilitates the development of a patient-centered case conceptualization consistent with the Nonadaptive Guilt and Shame (NAGS) model underlying TrIGR (Persons, 2012). The case conceptualization can be used to tailor the delivery of TrIGR to each individual client. For instance, a validated screening measure can be used to identify whether a client is engaging in risky substance use which can facilitate further discussion with the client, including how this behavior plays a role in maintaining NAGS and whether substance use needs to be limited during treatment. For example, the therapist might discuss not using substances prior to or immediately after therapy session or when completing homework assessments.

We recommend giving a short battery of self-report measures at the beginning of every other TrIGR session to monitor whether treatment is working and whether any modifications to the treatment plan need to be made. Research shows that sometimes therapists do not notice when patients are getting worse or not making progress in treatment when using clinical judgment alone (Fortney et al., 2017). Self-report measures can supplement clinical judgment in assessing how a client is doing in treatment and can signal to the therapist that further evaluation and/or adjustments to a treatment plan may be needed (Fortney et al., 2017). Measuring symptom severity regularly can also provide the opportunity for clinicians to refine their delivery of TrIGR by providing repeated opportunities to learn about their effectiveness when delivering this intervention.

Examples of validated measures

The list of assessment tools provided below is by no means an exhaustive one. For each category, we aimed to provide an example of at least one measure with strong psychometric properties that is particularly relevant to the treatment of trauma-related guilt and shame and common co-occurring problems. These are the measures we use in our own clinical work and research.

Assessing trauma-related guilt and shame

When choosing a measure to assess trauma-related guilt and/or shame, it can be helpful to consider the following:

(1) How the constructs of guilt and shame are defined. For example, some measures assess transient day-to-day guilt rather than the type of trauma-related guilt that is the target of TrIGR.

(2) How guilt and shame differ from one another.

(3) How state and trait forms of these emotions differ. "State" guilt or shame refers to the transitory experience of guilt or shame in response to specific experiences and "trait" guilt or shame refers to one's proclivity to generally experience guilt or shame. Measures of guilt and shame typically fall into one of these two broad categories (Tangney, 1996). Trauma-related guilt is generally considered state guilt (Kubany & Watson, 2003). A more extensive review of current conceptualizations and definitions of guilt and shame can be found in Chapter 2.

Currently, there are no gold standard clinician administered interviews to assess trauma-related guilt and/or shame. However, there are several validated self-report instruments, including the following:

The ***Trauma-Related Guilt Inventory*** (***TRGI***; Kubany et al., 1996) is a 32-item self-report questionnaire designed to measure guilt experienced as a result of surviving a traumatic event. The TRGI has three scales: (1) distress, (2) guilt cognitions, and (3) global guilt (frequency and intensity of posttraumatic guilt). The guilt cognitions scale consists of three subscales mapping onto common guilt-related beliefs that are targeted during TrIGR, including: (1) hindsight bias/responsibility, (2) lack of justification, and (3) wrongdoing. Developed over a series of seven studies in college students who experienced a traumatic event, female intimate partner violence survivors, and Vietnam Veterans, the TRGI exhibits good internal consistency, test-retest reliability, construct validity, and structural validity. Convergent validity was demonstrated for the three scales with other measures of guilt, PTSD, depression, self-esteem, shame, and social anxiety. The TRGI has also been found to weakly correlate with guilt elicited by commonplace everyday events.

The ***Trauma-Related Shame Inventory*** (***TRSI;*** Øktedalen, Hagtvet, Hoffart, Langkaas, & Smucker, 2014) is a 24-item self-report measure of internal and external trauma-related shame initially developed in a sample of 50 patients in treatment for PTSD. To our knowledge, the TRSI is the first shame scale to specifically assess trauma-related shame. Respondents are asked to rate how true a series of statements has been for them in the past week (e.g., "As a result of my traumatic experience, I have lost respect for myself"). While additional psychometric work is needed, the TRSI demonstrated promising construct validity in the initial development study.

Assessment of moral injury among Veteran clients

Veteran clients may have experienced moral injury as part of their trauma which may manifest as guilt and shame (see Chapters 2, 3, and 7 for more information). While the concept of moral injury has been around for quite some time, validated assessments designed to assess moral injury exposure are just beginning to emerge. While anyone can experience moral injury, current validated assessments are specific to military and Veteran populations. Examples of validated measures are as follows:

The ***Moral Injury Event Scale*** (***MIES***; Nash et al., 2013) is an 11-item measure of moral injury. Items ask whether the respondent believes he/she has engaged in behaviors inconsistent with their morals, witnessed others engaging in such behaviors, and/or felt betrayed. The MIES also includes items assessing commons symptoms of moral injury (e.g., guilt, shame, and distrust). Initial validation of the MIES in a military sample revealed good internal consistency and convergent validity (Nash et al., 2013).

The ***Moral Injury Questionnaire—Military Version*** (***MIQ-M***; Currier, Holland, Drescher, & Foy, 2015) is a 20-item self-report measure designed to assess exposure to committed or witnessed transgressive behaviors as well as perceived betrayal specifically in military populations. An initial study with a clinical sample found evidence of convergent validity (Currier et al., 2015). Of note while the MIQ-M asks about specific events, it does not asses common symptoms that follow moral injury, such as guilt and shame or spiritual crisis/meaning, and trust (see Jinkerson, 2016).

Assessment of other common posttraumatic symptoms and reactions

In addition to assessing trauma-related guilt and shame, we recommend assessing posttraumatic symptoms and distress that commonly accompany trauma-related guilt and shame, such as PTSD, depression, substance use disorders, and suicidality. Examples of validated diagnostic assessments are as follows:

Comprehensive Diagnostic Assessment

The ***Structured Clinical Interview for DSM-5*** (***SCID-5***; First, Williams, Karg, & Spitzer, 2015) is a clinician administered, semi-structured interview that assesses lifetime and current psychiatric diagnoses according to DSM-5 criteria. The SCID-5 clinical version is recommended for use in clinical or forensic settings, though research and clinical trial versions are also available. Information regarding the reliability and validity of SCID-5 is not yet available, although the reliability and validity of previous versions of the SCID were evaluated in a number of studies and summaries of these results are freely available (see www.SCID4.org). Each version of the SCID-5 is available for purchase (www.SCID5.org).

Posttraumatic Stress Disorder (PTSD)

The ***Clinician-Administered PTSD Scale for DSM-5*** (***CAPS***; Blake et al., 1995) is a 30-item structured diagnostic interview corresponding to DSM-5. It is widely regarded as the gold standard for determining a diagnosis of PTSD. Respondents are asked to select the trauma or traumas that cause them the most problems now and PTSD symptoms related to this event are assessed. Categorical (diagnostic) or dimensional scoring of PTSD (severity) can be used. The CAPS also includes questions assessing the onset and duration of symptoms, subjective distress, the impact of symptoms on social and occupational functioning, and overall response validity. Current (past month) and lifetime versions are available for use when diagnosing PTSD. A past week version can also be used to assess PTSD symptom severity. The full interview takes approximately 45–60 min to administer. Information regarding the reliability and validity of the current version of the CAPS is being collected. The previous version of the CAPS, corresponding to DSM-IV, was evaluated in survivors of a number of forms of trauma and consistently demonstrated high levels of internal consistency, good interrater reliability, and excellent convergent validity. Request for this assessment can be made at: https://www.ptsd.va.gov/professional/assessment/adult-int/caps.asp#obtain.

The ***PTSD Checklist–5*** (***PCL-5***; Weathers et al., 2013) is a widely used self-report assessment of PTSD symptom severity. It can be used to screen clients for PTSD, make provisional PTSD diagnoses, as well as to monitor symptom change over the course of treatment. The symptom checklist consists of 20 items corresponding to DSM-5 PTSD diagnostic criteria. Respondents rate how much they are bothered by each PTSD symptom. There are two additional versions of the PCL-5: (1) the symptom checklist that includes a brief assessment of DSM-5 Criterion A (the traumatic event) and (2) the symptom checklist that includes the Life Events Checklist for DSM-5 (LEC-5) and an extended Criterion A assessment. Currently, the psychometric properties of the PCL-5 have been evaluated in trauma-exposed college students, treatment seeking military service members, and Veterans. However, the previous versions of the PCL (corresponding to DSM-IV) were validated in numerous populations and also showed excellent psychometric properties (for a review see Wilkins, Lang, & Norman, 2011). This measure is further described and available via the Department of Veteran Affairs National Center for PTSD's website: https://www.ptsd.va.gov/professional/assessment/adult-sr/ptsd-checklist.asp.

Depression

The ***Patient Health Questionnaire-9*** (*PHQ-9*; Kroenke & Spitzer, 2002) is a 9-item self-report scale assessing and monitoring the severity and frequency of depression symptoms over a 2-week period. It is among the most widely used self-report depression measures in clinical populations. The PHQ-9 is based directly on the diagnostic criteria for major depressive disorder and is consistent with DSM-5 criteria. The PHQ-9 was originally validated in thousands of primary care patients and obstetrics-gynecology patients and has since been evaluated in psychiatric, behavioral health, and geriatric populations and is available in a number of languages. As the criteria for major depression did not change in DSM-5, previous validation studies remain reflective of the psychometric properties of this measure. The PHQ-9 can be accessed at: http://www.phqscreeners.com.

Suicidality

The ***Columbia-Suicide Severity Rating Scale*** (*C-SSRS*; Posner et al., 2008) is a standardized clinician administered risk assessment that can be used to assess a full range of suicidal thoughts, behaviors, and risk factors. The C-SSRS can be used to identify whether someone is at risk for suicide, measure severity and immediacy of risk, and identify forms of support needed by a client. Administration takes less than 5 min. The C-SSRS consistently demonstrates excellent psychometric properties across a range of adolescent and adult populations and is available in a number of languages. Information regarding this measure and its psychometric support can be found at: http://www.cssrs.columbia.edu.

Substance Use

The ***Alcohol Use Disorder Identification Test*** (*AUDIT*; Reinert & Allen, 2002; Saunders, Aasland, Babor, De La Fuente, & Grant, 1993) is a 10-item self-report measure that can be used to screen and monitor excessive drinking, specific consequences of alcohol use, and alcohol use disorder. It was developed using data from a multinational study conducted by the World Health Organization in primary care settings. It has since been used in a range of primary care studies, epidemiological studies, and research involving hospital patients, and has been translated into a number of languages. The AUDIT-Consumption (AUDIT-C; Bush, 1998) is an abbreviated version of the AUDIT consisting of the first three items. Research examining this measure in relation to DSM-5 alcohol use disorder criteria is ongoing. This measure is further described and available at: www.auditscreen.org.

The ***Drug Use Disorder Identification Test*** (*DUDIT*; Berman, Bergman, Palmstierna, & Schlyter, 2005) is an 11-item self-report measure designed as a drug use disorder screen parallel to the above-described AUDIT. It can be used to screen for and monitor problematic drug use, drug use disorder, and certain related problems and has been translated into a number of languages. The DUDIT has been examined in psychiatric populations, addiction treatment samples, and criminal justice settings prior to the release of DSM-5. A manual is available and can be requested from the instrument developer (see Berman et al., 2005).

The ***Brief Addiction Monitor*** (*BAM*; Cacciola et al., 2013) is a 17-item multidimensional questionnaire developed to assess substance use-related behaviors. The BAM queries substance use, recovery, and treatment engagement over the past month. The BAM yields three subscores: Recovery Protection, Physical and Psychological Problems, and Substance Use and Risk. To date, the psychometric properties of this measure have been evaluated in Veterans enrolled in Veterans Affairs outpatient treatment programs and have shown strong psychometric properties (Cacciola et al., 2013; Nelson, Young, & Chapman, 2014).

Assessment of additional recovery-focused outcomes

Evaluating recovery-oriented outcomes such as psychosocial functioning and quality of life may also be clinically indicated and useful when delivering TrIGR. Examples of validated measures are as follows:

Quality of Life

The ***World Health Organization Quality of Life*** (*WHO-QOL-BREF*; World Health Organization, 1998) is a 26-item self-report measure of physical, psychological, social relationships, and environmental quality of life. The WHO-QOL-BREF was developed by the World Health Organization as part of an international effort to develop a cross-cultural quality of life self-report tool. This measure is further described and available at: www.who.int.

Psychosocial Functioning

The ***Inventory of Psychosocial Functioning*** (*IPF*; Bovin et al., 2018) is a new 80-item self-report measure of PTSD-related functional impairment in the past 30 days related to relationships, work, parenting, education, and general daily functioning. The initial development study was conducted in a sample of Veterans and active duty military personnel. In this study, the IPF demonstrated promising internal consistency and correlated highly with other established measures of functional impairment.

Of note, some of these instruments are publicly available while others may need to be purchased. We recommend clinicians research any costs that may be associated with using an assessment tool in routine clinical practice.

PART 2 PREPARATION AND CASE RELATED CONSIDERATIONS

CHAPTER 6

Preparing clients for TrIGR

Clients struggling with guilt and shame following trauma often have sophisticated strategies to avoid talking about and thinking about their traumatic events. Because Trauma Informed Guilt Reduction (TrIGR) therapy asks clients to address their trauma, guilt, and shame head on, we believe it is important to address possible ambivalence about doing so prior to beginning the therapy and throughout therapy as needed. This chapter covers strategies to help clients engage in TrIGR by helping them decrease avoidance and increase motivation for the treatment. We suggest strategies to use before starting TrIGR and also during TrIGR if it seems like a client's motivation for treatment is faltering.

Motivational interviewing prior to starting TrIGR to prepare clients for therapy

Miller and Rollnick (2013) define motivational interviewing as a collaborative conversation between the therapist and the client and recommend it as a strategy to enhance a client's personal motivation and commitment to change. The process of change is complex and can be emotionally difficult. Even clients who want to feel less guilt and shame can also feel ambivalent about changing. While clients may want to feel better, part of them may believe they deserve to suffer for what they did. Or, they may believe they are already too overwhelmed by their symptoms and distress to focus on their trauma.

Motivational interviewing was originally developed to help clients reduce alcohol or drug use. It is now used for a wide variety of medical and mental health-related behavior change, including engagement in psychotherapy (Miller & Rollnick, 2013; Seal et al., 2012). Although motivational interviewing techniques can be interwoven into various stages of treatment,

Trauma Informed Guilt Reduction Therapy
https://doi.org/10.1016/B978-0-12-814780-1.00006-X

a motivational enhancement session before starting TrIGR can be a helpful technique for preparing clients to confront their trauma and appraise their guilt and shame. A motivational enhancement session may move clients toward the changes that they want to make.

A key concept in motivational interviewing is that ambivalence is a normal and natural part of recovery. Clients struggling with guilt and shame from trauma often demonstrate ambivalence about engaging in a treatment that will address their guilt and shame so directly. For this reason, having a session before starting TrIGR dedicated to exploring the client's ambivalence, the function of their guilt, and what is and is not working for them in how they are handling their guilt and distress can be critical in treatment engagement.

We recommend using this pre-TrIGR session to assess motivation and establish treatment goals. In this session, we use a semi-structured approach to explore the client's readiness to engage in a guilt-focused intervention. The goals within the session are to (1) build rapport and introduce non-adaptive guilt and shame (NAGS), (2) assess symptoms and problems, (3) openly explore potential barriers to treatment (e.g., substance use, competing time commitments), (4) identify motivators to engage in treatment (external and internal) and identify client-specific treatment goals, and (5) promote client choice in moving forward with treatment. Below we describe strategies we use to meet these goals. Motivational interviewing concepts are embedded throughout this session. These include: (a) expression of empathy, (b) reflections, (c) open ended questions, (d) promoting self-efficacy, (e) rolling with resistance, and (f) developing discrepancy between values and current behaviors. For additional information on these concepts refer to *Motivational Interviewing: Helping People Change* (Miller & Rollnick, 2013).

(1) Building rapport and introduce NAGS

The therapist takes an active role to create a safe, warm, and nonjudgmental environment. This is crucial in all trauma work but is especially important when processing NAGS. Talking about the source of guilt and shame can be extremely difficult for clients. Many therapists have reported that they ease into discussing difficult topics, such as guilt and shame, over many sessions, and wait for the client to feel comfortable. However, we suggest that the therapist actively engage in conversations about guilt, self-blame, and shame during the pretreatment session not only to set the stage for guilt-focused discussions that will occur throughout the brief protocol, but also to provide immediate evidence to the client that you will not collude with their avoidance nor will you judge them negatively.

> *Thank you for coming in today to discuss how your guilt may be affecting your life and for considering engaging in a guilt and shame focused intervention. We will spend most of the session going through questions to understand what is bringing you into treatment now and to understand your goals for therapy. We will also talk about the things that might get in the way of you being able to do a treatment focusing on trauma-related guilt. These may be things that make it difficult to come in every week or do the work outside of session. I will also spend some time describing the treatment to you and answering your questions to help you determine if you would like to move forward. How does that sound?*

> *Can you tell me ways in which the trauma has disrupted your life?*

> *Can you tell me how your feelings of guilt have been negatively affecting your life?*

> *What positive things might happen if we were able to reduce the guilt and shame you feel?*

(2) Assess symptoms and problems

Clients may present with a variety of symptoms and struggles that have been exacerbated as a result of experiencing trauma-related guilt and shame. Therapists should ask the client how their guilt is negatively influencing their current beliefs about themselves, others, and the world. It is also helpful to assess how their symptoms may affect their ability to engage in treatment (more on that below).

> *In addition to guilt, some people who have experienced traumatic events describe struggling with depressed mood, anxiety, anger, grief, and loss. Have you noticed these feelings or other reactions? How do you think that your feelings of guilt affect these emotions?*

> *Sometimes people feel worse before they feel better in treatment. What might that belike for you? Do you think that would affect your engagement in treatment?*

(3) Explore barriers of change

The therapist should spend a large portion of the session identifying and discussing potential barriers to change. Talk with the client about the things that might get in the way of being able to do psychotherapy for trauma-related guilt. Explore the situations that may prevent the client from coming into session on a weekly basis and/or completing between session assignments. Openly discuss both practical barriers (e.g., difficulty with transportation, starting a new job) and emotion-based barriers (e.g., emotional avoidance, beliefs that the client deserves to suffer). Further explore any barriers clients identify and ask them to generate ideas for how they will overcome the barriers.

How the therapist's responds to the client's ambivalence can set the stage as to whether clients will share ambivalence they may feel later in treatment. We try to convey that ambivalence is a normal and healthy part of the recovery process and that our role in this session is to help clients decide whether to engage in TrIGR, not to talk them into doing so.

> *Within TrIGR, you would be encouraged to look directly at the situation or situations that have led you to feel guilt and distress. You and I would talk about your traumatic event and the thoughts and feelings behind your guilt and shame. Treatment requires time and effort, consistent attendance, and completing assignments between our meetings. We would work toward the goals we agreed to, and you would be an active participant in session. Is there anything that may get in the way for you of being able to do any of this?*
>
> *Let's take some time to better understand some of the reasons why it might be hard to engage in an intervention focusing on guilt and shame. What concerns do you have about doing this?*
>
> *What are the risks of working on your guilt? What might be the benefits?*
>
> *Sometimes people feel that their guilt serves an important role for them and that they should feel guilt or shame. Is this something that you relate to? What are some of the pros of feeling guilt? What are some of the cons of experiencing guilt in this way?*

Practical barriers are often easier to discuss with the client. For example, if the client is starting a new job, we may recommend that the client start treatment once they know their new schedule. Addressing ambivalence related to emotional barriers can be more difficult. Most clients are likely to experience some level of ambivalence with the idea of engaging in treatment, confronting their avoidance behaviors, or engaging in a discussion related to their trauma or to their guilt and shame.

Below are several examples of common types of emotion-based barriers to treatment and some suggestions for how to address these.

(a) *Fears of talking about the trauma:* Clients can have different reasons for not wanting to talk about their trauma, and sometimes they do not even fully understand why talking about the trauma is difficult. Helping clients understand their fears can help put them at ease. For example, clients may want to avoid intense negative emotions, like guilt and shame, fearing they would not be able to handle them, or that they would be compelled by their emotions to act in negative ways. Clients may be ambivalent about disclosing specific aspects of trauma because they feel ashamed, or because they are concerned that they or someone else will be arrested, or because of their desire to keep an oath that they took with someone (e.g., promising their abuse perpetrator that they would not tell anyone). For additional information as to how to address some of these concerns refer to Chapter 7.

(b) *Negative beliefs about oneself:* Our TrIGR clients are prone to experience negative beliefs about their actions during the time of the trauma and about themselves in general. These beliefs can make them ambivalent about sharing their trauma with you or others. When clients have thoughts like the following, they often believe other people will come to the same negative conclusions about them. It is helpful to ask clients directly about these (1) to allow them to see that these are common beliefs that are symptoms of posttraumatic distress (and therefore may not be accurate) and (2) to witness that you do not judge them the way they believe they will be judged.

I should have/should not have done.

I'm a monster.

I'm a failure.

If my family knew about what happened they would leave me.

I don't deserve to feel better.

(c) *Hopelessness, doubt, and skepticism:* Due to longstanding emotional distress, clients may be skeptical that treatment will help them feel better. Although some clients may overtly discuss these doubts with you, often the therapist will pick up on these beliefs through more subtle cues. The following are common expressions of this kind of ambivalence:

I have a lot going on right now, I'm not sure if this is the right time for treatment.

I don't think I'll ever stop feeling this way, there really isn't a point in trying to workon this.

(d) *Social stigma:* Clients may believe that getting mental health treatment will stigmatize them and thus is not worth it (Corrigan, 2004; Mittal et al., 2013). Often, just bringing such beliefs to light can help deflate the stigma enough for a client to engage in treatment. Sometimes, you will need to address stigma more explicitly with Socratic questioning.

(e) *Guilt as a function to connect to a value system:* Many times, clients come to believe that having guilt and shame is necessary or even helpful in some way. These beliefs can sound like the following.

I owe it to those who lost their lives to not let go of this pain.

This is my way to not forget.

If I believe it was not my fault, I will let my guard down and I'll be hurt again.

We address these beliefs in great depth during TrIGR. In this pretreatment session we may (1) praise clients for their willingness to bear the burden of holding onto their NAGS in the service of remembering or honoring others, or to prevent a similar trauma from happening again; and (2) asking clients if they are willing to keep an open mind about the possibility of having other ways to achieve these ends.

(4) Identify motivators to change and establish treatment goals

Throughout this session, we try to understand why clients want to engage in a treatment focusing on guilt and what their motivation is for coming into treatment now. When establishing treatment goals, it is important to help clients identify both short-term treatment goals (e.g., decrease distress, feel less guilt) and long-term goals (e.g., have a better relationship with family).

People who go into therapy understanding their goals and their concerns have the best chance of being successful. So far, we have addressed some of your concerns about doing TrIGR. Now let's take some time to better understand why you are here and identify some of your goals for therapy.

What would you like to change in your life now?

Are there things that your family and friends can do that you have a difficult time doing? In what ways do you think this treatment might help you do those things?

It sounds like this trauma and carrying this guilt and shame have affected you for quite some time. Why did you decide to come into treatment now rather than 3 months ago or 3 months from now?

Highlight discrepancies between the client's identified goals and values and how they are currently living their lives as a result of experiencing NAGS.

I can see you feel that working on your guilt will be difficult. However, it also seems like the way that you are feeling is affecting your ability to maintain relationships. How might working on your guilt and shame help you develop a stronger connection with your family?

(5) Promote client choice

Therapeutic change happens when someone decides to change, not when someone is told to change (Le, Doctor, Zoellner, & Feeny, 2014). Utilize the remainder of the session to briefly describe TrIGR and any other options you and the client are considering. This is a good opportunity to instill hope and confidence in the client's ability to benefit from TrIGR.

At the end of the session provide a summary of what you and the client discussed over the course of the session, including the client's reasons, pros, and cons for engaging in TrIGR. Do not assume that the client would like to proceed with treatment. At the end of the session ask the client if they would like to proceed.

If the client continues to express ambivalence, you could ask this follow-up question:

What will happen if you choose to not work on your guilt?

Addressing ambivalence throughout TrIGR

Clients may experience ambivalence during treatment. They may miss sessions, not complete assignments, or not fully engage in session. Brief motivational enhancement can be used throughout TrIGR to understand the source of the ambivalence and to address it.

Integrating motivational enhancement strategies into TrIGR sessions is similar to using these strategies in the pretreatment session. The therapist continues to emphasize collaborative communication, demonstrate confidence in the intervention, exhibit confidence in the client, and normalize the client's ambivalence. The therapist encourages the client to reidentify their short-term and long-term goals, consider consequences of not addressing their NAGS, and weigh the potential benefits they may experience if NAGS is reduced. The therapist may also highlight the client's accomplishments thus far, like sharing the trauma story or identifying guilt cognitions that cause distress. It can be helpful to emphasize the discrepancy between what clients are feeling and what they have accomplished and to remind them that therapy is a process and that any long-term benefit takes time and is not achieved linearly, that there are bumps along the way, but that these bumps are not indications that the client is not able to complete the treatment or will not continue to benefit. Lastly, the therapist can continue to check in with the client about new barriers and encourage the client to identify ways to overcome these barriers. The therapist and the client can engage in problem solving around the barriers together.

> *I've noticed that you seem more distant this week and you brought up that this treatment may be too difficult for you. Let's take a moment to revisit your reasons for working on your guilt.*

> *It sounds as if you feel you aren't getting better. Let's check in and see where you are with meeting your goals.*

> *Despite feeling some distress this week, it sounds like you have a lot of reasons to continue to work on reducing your guilt. I know you have had a difficult time listening to the session recording. What might be helpful this week? Would you be open to having your spouse remind you?*

PART 2 PREPARATION AND CASE RELATED CONSIDERATIONS

CHAPTER 7

Considerations for therapists

In this chapter, we talk about some of the unique issues that may arise for specific trauma types such as combat and interpersonal traumas. We also address questions that therapists often ask us when first using Trauma Informed Guilt Reduction (TrIGR) therapy, such as "What if my client abuses drugs or alcohol?," "What if my client has religious beliefs that contribute to their guilt?," or "What if my client wants to make a reparative gesture to try to make amends for what happened?"

Working with military service members: A focus on moral injury

Military experiences in the context of a client's core values

In 2009, Litz and colleagues coined the term *moral injury* to describe the psychological conflict between an individual's personal value system and engagement in activities associated with death and destruction during war (Litz et al., 2009). The underlying core values of the military (e.g., honor, courage, strength, responsibility, integrity, esprit de corps) reinforce resilience and cohesion during military service and are infused in all areas of military life: physical discipline, mental discipline, character, and combat readiness (Yi, 2004). These core values are critical to survival in a combat zone. However, they may interfere with healthy recovery from trauma and contribute to someone's distress. For example, "I am responsible for those with whom I serve" can turn into "I should have been able to keep everyone in my unit alive." In TrIGR, we identify and help clients examine such extreme and unrealistic interpretations of military values.

Exposure to losses, injury, and death are common for service members in wartime and are traumas that can lead to moral injury. In addition to

https://doi.org/10.1016/B978-0-12-814780-1.00007-1

the tangible losses of life, service members may experience existential or symbolic losses, such as loss of religious/spiritual faith, loss of meaning, loss of innocence, and loss of self-worth. The experience of these losses, both tangible and symbolic, can contribute to difficulties finding a sense of purpose and increased moral injury and can directly contribute to post-traumatic guilt and shame. For some clients, it may be easier, more socially acceptable, or more in line with a warrior mindset to experience guilt and shame rather than grieve these losses. Processing guilt related to traumatic loss can be even more challenging if one of its functions has been to protect against the experience of grief. With regard to loss, power and control is a common theme that is explored within the TrIGR protocol. Loss of control in a situation, regardless of the reason, can also lead to a great deal of guilt. The following are examples of military experiences that may cause moral injury and may reinforce guilt and shame cognitions:

(a) Changes in the rules of engagement or orders (e.g., changes from orders to fire at everyone to only fire when fired upon). This can make rules seem arbitrary and result in your client doubting themselves for having followed the orders they did.

(b) Learning of negative outcomes even after taking an action in good faith (e.g., learning that a bombing resulted in killing women and children rather than the enemy).

(c) Not having adequate information (e.g., seeing a fellow service member medically evacuated after an injury and not knowing if the person lived or died).

(d) Failing to act or to report (e.g., witnessing a member of leadership engaging in unnecessary hostile force toward prisoners resulting in injury).

(e) Witnessing and/or engaging in atrocious acts (e.g., killing/harming others).

Military life and culture

It is very helpful to have some understanding of military life, values, and culture to help clients who were or are in the military. Such knowledge gives therapists more credibility with the client, but also helps the therapist understand the nuances of why someone is suffering with guilt and shame and possibly moral injury. For example, military culture may lead a client to believe that they were responsible for everyone else in their unit at the time of the trauma, even if realistically this was not possible. Understanding the job someone had in the military during the trauma is also critical to understanding someone's sense of guilt and responsibility. For therapists who are new to treating Veterans or service members, there are many helpful online resources. These include:

- The Veterans Affairs Community Provider Toolkit: https://www.mentalhealth.va.gov/communityproviders/military_resources.asp
- The Department of Defense (DoD)/Uniformed Services University Military Culture Course: https://deploymentpsych.org/military-culture-course-modules
- Military Culture Courses by PsychArmor: https://psycharmor.org/military-culture-school/
- Posttraumatic stress disorder (PTSD) and Military Culture: https://www.ptsd.va.gov/professional/continuing_ed/military_culture.asp

Some specific aspects of military culture that will be relevant if using the TrIGR protocol with service members or Veterans are noted below.

It is helpful when conducting TrIGR with a service member or Veteran to understand the duties and expectations of the military job they had at the time their trauma occurred. Some questions to ask are: "What was your job? For what and whom were you responsible?" Over our time treating service members and Veterans using TrIGR, we have recognized some common themes among those with certain roles or professions within the military. We describe these below and for each theme, we also provide examples of the common types of nonadaptive guilt and/or shame that may go with these. These are discussed in greater detail in the TrIGR manual.

(a) *Corpsmen/medics* take an oath to care for all of those who are injured. Although corpsmen and medics may have limited medical training (i.e., they are not medical doctors), while in a combat zone, it is not uncommon for them to feel pressure to help and/or save everyone; and subsequently they can feel severe guilt if someone in their care dies.

    Common types of nonadaptive guilt:

    - *Incompetence/superman/superwoman guilt*
    - *Overestimation of knowledge and control*

(b) Those in *officer/leadership roles* are expected to provide direction and guidance to other service members. Service members in leadership positions are often faced with life or death decisions. Decisions that lead to death or harm to subordinates or other negative outcomes can lead to a great deal of guilt (even when there may not have been an option that led to a better outcome).

Common types of nonadaptive guilt:

- *Negligence/betrayal/abandonment guilt*
- *Incompetence/superman/superwoman guilt*
- *Overestimation of knowledge and control*

(c) Members of *small teams* often develop a deep connection with each other. Such teams may have multiple deployments and whether a great deal of adversity together; therefore, losses within small teams are often felt very deeply. Some small teams may be tasked with specialty missions and may be more likely to witness and/or participate in atrocities.

Common types of nonadaptive guilt:

- *Negligence/betrayal/abandonment guilt*
- *Survivor or leaving guilt*
- *Atrocity guilt*

(d) Individuals from *elite groups* are trained to be the "best of the best" and to overcome extreme obstacles. Similar to small teams, elite groups may be exposed to atrocious acts (e.g., harsh punishment, hand-to-hand combat, and death of civilians including women and children). Members of elite groups may be guarded when they come to therapy because their work required them to disclose little information. Thus, they may require additional rapport building to establish trust prior to engaging in trauma-focused treatment. It is also possible that their traumas occurred during classified events, so they may not be able to (or may not feel they are able to) share parts of what happened with you. (See "Inability to Disclose Aspects of the Trauma" below for suggestions on how to deal with such situations.)

Common types of nonadaptive guilt:

- *Negligence/betrayal/abandonment guilt*
- *Incompetence/superman/superwoman guilt*
- *Overestimation of knowledge and control*
- *Survivor or leaving guilt*
- *Atrocity guilt*

Inability to disclose aspects of the trauma

A service member may not be willing or able to disclose aspects of a traumatic event. This may be because the trauma involved classified information or possibly because the client made a promise or oath to the military or another service member not to talk about the incident. In such situations, the therapist needs to explore whether TrIGR is the appropriate treatment since a main component of the therapy is to debrief the traumatic event. The therapist can remind the client of the limits of therapist-client confidentiality. For example, in most cases, a therapist does not break confidentiality to report past events unless someone is presently in danger (e.g., a child). The therapist should take as much time as needed to answer the client's questions regarding the limits of confidentiality. Additionally, we find it helpful to explore with the client exactly how much would need to be disclosed to effectively process the trauma. It is possible that the client may be able to share adequate details without disclosing the exact battle, location, or other identifiable details. It is not necessary for the client to disclose every detail of the trauma for guilt processing to be effective (e.g., names, places, dates), but rather the context of the trauma (e.g., death of a friend, how long the individual was awake, length of time of the firefight). It may also be possible for the service member or Veteran to seek and get permission from their supervisor or a higher-ranking official to discuss some of the details of their trauma in the context of treatment. Finally, we encourage therapists to use motivational enhancement strategies to help the client explore pros and cons of engaging in trauma-focused work. It is possible that the benefits to the client of engaging in treatment will outweigh concerns regarding discussing an incident. See Chapter 6 for suggestions on how to use motivational interviewing techniques in regard to TrIGR. Ultimately, it is up to clients to decide how much to disclose and whether to proceed with TrIGR, especially if there may be legal ramifications for disclosure.

Clients who intentionally perpetrated a trauma

Many clients tell us they purposely perpetrated harm. Clients who feel guilt and shame about a trauma, and clients who experience moral injury, often believe they purposely perpetrated harm whether or not this is actually true. Many times, someone's intention falls into a gray zone. For example, someone drove while intoxicated and caused an accident that caused a death. While clearly they hold responsibility for what happened, their intention is not as obvious. Other times, the intention is more obvious, such as when a Veteran client tells us he went back into a village after a battle and killed civilians. The client tells us he did so in a state of immense grief and anger after having lost people he cared about like brothers in the battle and that what he did has haunted him ever since. In both cases, we would consider TrIGR to be a viable treatment option because with TrIGR, our focus is not whether someone had a role in perpetrating the trauma but rather whether they feel guilt and shame about their role in the trauma now. Our goal is to help our clients come to terms with their past actions so they can go forward living a more meaningful life and live to their best potential. If a client presents with guilt and shame, it is worth further assessment to see if TrIGR is an appropriate intervention.

It is important to remember that the goal of TrIGR is never to talk a client out of feeling guilty or ashamed for something they have done. We want to be clear with therapists as well as clients that guilt may be appropriate and may serve an adaptive function, and the purpose of TrIGR is not to get rid of this emotion. As such, we never say to a client that the trauma was "not your fault," or that the client had no responsibility in the event. Rather, we help the client in placing their role in the trauma in the broader context of what occurred and to consider all of the factors that contributed to the outcome, so they can come to their own, more accurate, conclusions.

In TrIGR, we take the client through a series of exercises to recall the broader context of what occurred during the trauma. Through the exercises, we have the client consider the context of the event and all of the contributing factors and then reflect on their intentions at the time. This is the essence of Module 2 of the protocol. We find this process often helps clients realize that they did not intend to cause harm. For those who find they did intend to cause harm, they are better able to consider what else was driving them at the time. They often worry that because they perpetrated the trauma, they are evil and will perpetrate more harm if they do not suffer from guilt and shame. TrIGR helps them explore whether that is true, or whether in fact the circumstances at the time of the trauma were so extreme and painful and outside of the scope of normal life (e.g., losing many loved ones in a battle), that how they acted then is in fact not an indication of who they are at their core and what they will do in any given future situation.

Let us consider a scenario that may be very challenging for some therapists and clients to process: a parent who causes harm to their child due to excessive physical punishment or neglect. We would be hard-pressed to find anyone who would argue that the parent should not feel guilt or shame about their behavior in such a case. However, would it serve this parent, their child, their other children, us, or society at large, for them to continue to experience NAGS? With NAGS, this parent would be more likely continue to behave in ways that have interpersonal and societal costs (e.g., anger, aggression, violence, substance use, and impaired functioning at home, at work, and in society). TrIGR, in this case could assist the parent in halting the NAGS cycle and accessing and living their values moving forward. In a case like this, a client would likely continue to feel guilt and shame following therapy. But recall that guilt and shame are not in themselves reason for intervention. It is NAGS that TrIGR targets. If clients can step out of the NAGS cycle, they can allow their choices and behaviors to be informed by their emotions of guilt and shame as opposed to be suppressed by them. In TrIGR, clients have the chance to recognize that while they have acted in ways that go against their values, which cannot be undone, they can express their remorse and values in ways other than continuing NAGS (which, ironically, may increase the likelihood that they will not live according to their values). In TrIGR, clients who have caused harm confront, rather than avoid, their justified guilt and shame, allowing them to make values-based decisions moving forward.

Survivors of interpersonal trauma

Survivors of interpersonal traumas can experience trauma-related guilt and shame for many reasons. A few common ones are because they believe that the abuse was their fault, that they deserved the abuse, or, in the case of repeated or ongoing interpersonal abuse, that they should have stopped it or left sooner. There are many reasons why this occurs (see Chapter 2). For one, when the abuse is perpetrated by someone the victim depends on in some way (sometimes called betrayal trauma), the victim may place blame for the abuse on themselves by concluding they caused it or deserved it. This helps them find a way to maintain a relationship they depend on, but can leave them with NAGS. Victims of interpersonal trauma often do not report the abuse afterward (Jonzon & Lindblad, 2004; Smith et al., 2000), and this appears to be especially likely for betrayal trauma survivors (Malloy, Lyon, & Quas, 2007; Tang, Freyd, & Wang, 2008). Additionally, interpersonal abuse may automatically produce a shame response, with its accompanying subservience and deference behaviors that can reduce the likelihood of further maltreatment in the moment (Gilbert & Andrews, 1998). These are some of the many reasons that survivors of interpersonal trauma may experience NAGS. Importantly, these also offer alternative explanations to survivors who have come to believe that they "did nothing" to stop or prevent the abuse, or "chose to stay" with their abuser.

Sexual abuse, one type of interpersonal trauma, has additional layers that can contribute to trauma-related guilt and shame for both women and men. For one, it is common for victims of sexual assault to experience some physiological arousal during the assault, and later when reminded of it. Physiological arousal is in part a reflexive response to being physically stimulated in certain areas of the body or having the expectation that sex is ensuing whether or not the stimulation or arousal is desired (Levin & van Berlo, 2004). This physiological arousal can lead the victim to feel confused and question whether they somehow desired, attracted, tolerated, or even enjoyed being abused, which fuels trauma-related guilt and shame (Dorais, 2002). In addition, many sexual trauma survivors report having sexual fantasies that involve force or victimization (Briere, Smiljanich, & Henschel, 1994), and feel guilt and shame as a result of this experience (Westerlund, 1992; Wilson & Wilson, 2008). An explanation for such arousal comes from behavioral psychology. Specifically, the automatic physiological response can become paired with any part of the abuse scenario, particularly if it is repeated, and can be elicited when exposed to reminders of the abuse, through direct exposure or imagining or thinking about it (Abel, 1974; Martin & Pear, 1999).

It is also common for people who are sexually or physically abused to experience a peri-traumatic (i.e., during the trauma) freeze response (Burgess & Holmstrom, 1976; Rizvi, Kayen, Gutner, Griffin, & Resick, 2008). This is an automatic response similar to fight or flight that can be adaptive at the time of trauma. For example, it may keep someone from getting hurt further. However, it is often interpreted by trauma survivors as passivity, acceptance, and even desirability, and for these reasons, clients often report feeling guilty and ashamed because they froze at the time of the trauma (Galliano, Noble, Travis, & Puechl, 1993).

Men may be particularly susceptible to NAGS following sexual trauma because being sexually victimized is incongruent with aspects of masculine identity, which is based on ideals that men should exhibit strength, power, and control (Murdoch, Pryor, Polusny, & Gackstetter, 2007). Assault by a woman can contribute further to NAGS because of societal beliefs that men should be stronger than women (Kelly, Wood, Gonzalez, MacDonald, & Waterman, 2002). Because such beliefs are common, if the victim tells others of the sexual trauma, they may react with disbelief or other negative reactions, which can then lead to more self-blame (Davies, 2002; Ullman, 2002).

In Module 1 of TrIGR, we include psychoeducation about why peri- and posttraumatic responses, such as freezing, self-blame, having positive views of the perpetrator, or physiological arousal, may be adaptive (by helping survival) at the time of the trauma. This helps to set the stage for debriefing guilt and shame in Module 2.

Finally, it is not uncommon for individuals who are abused by someone close to them to promise their perpetrator that they will keep the abuse secret. While survivors might have mixed feelings about their perpetrator, they may feel guilty about disclosing the abuse, even in therapy. They may feel like they are betraying their abuser (e.g., a parent or partner) and even themselves. Some of the strategies for working with military service members who feel conflicted about discussing their trauma could apply here. These include reminding the client about therapist-client confidentiality, explaining the possibility of effectively engaging in TrIGR without disclosing every detail of the trauma, and utilizing motivational interviewing techniques including reviewing the client's pros and cons for completing treatment. In terms of confidentiality, the client should be reminded that a therapist would need to break confidentiality if someone is presently in danger (e.g., when the client's child abuse perpetrator is alive and currently has access to children).

Working with comorbid alcohol and substance use disorders

Problematic use of alcohol or drugs is common among those who experience posttraumatic distress (Kessler, 1995). Among Veterans, substance use may be an expression of self-injurious behavior, a common component of moral injury. Historically, people with addiction were considered too fragile for trauma-focused treatments such as TrIGR (Back et al., 2015). This recommendation was often based upon clinicians' fears that clients would relapse to drugs, emotionally decompensate, or experience an increase in cravings. Due to these clinician fears, clients often received sequential treatment first for substance use and then for other trauma-related problems. Unfortunately, because relapse is common among individuals with addiction, many clients never progressed to trauma-focused treatment (Norman & Hamblen, 2017). However, a growing number of studies have shown that people with active substance use disorders, even those still using but working to cut down or quit, can handle and benefit from trauma-focused treatment (Foa et al., 2013; Simpson, Lehavot, & Petrakis, 2017). Based on this research, as well as research showing that treating PTSD also helps people recover from addiction, concurrent treatment, where interventions to address addiction and posttraumatic distress are offered at the same time, are now recommended (Department of Veterans Affairs & Department of Defense, 2017).

Use of alcohol or other drugs should not rule out engaging in TrIGR. However, therapists should assess a client's substance use prior to treatment to develop a thorough understanding of the client's current and past use, including all the elements we list below. Many clients will not disclose their use unless their therapist asks about it directly. Discussions about alcohol and drug use can elicit feelings of guilt and shame for clients. Chapter 5 includes recommendations for validated assessments for alcohol and drug use. Other considerations when assessing alcohol and drug use include:

(a) Type of substance (e.g., alcohol, marijuana, overuse of prescription medications)

(b) Most recent period and length of sobriety

(c) Internal and/or external triggers that prompted lapse/relapse

(d) Frequency and amount of use (e.g., how many days per week/month; two beers on weekdays, binge-episodes of six beers on weekends)

(e) Client's goals regarding their use right now (e.g., abstinence and cutting down)

(f) Willingness to set goals to reduce their use

(g) Factors to help clients reach their goals

(h) Factors that might get in the way of meeting goals

In addition, when assessing for problematic alcohol and substance use, it is important to understand the function or reasons for use (e.g., to be around people, to decrease distress, to sleep better, to avoid certain feelings or thoughts, to manage pain). Some clients may use out of habit or for social connection; however, among those who have experienced trauma, it is common to use substances to suppress or avoid distressing feelings associated with the trauma. This is referred to as self-medication (Khantzian, 1985). Clients may be using alcohol and other substances to get away from the distress of their guilt and shame (Street, Gibson, & Holohan, 2005). In some cases, clients may use substances as a form of self-punishment. Unfortunately, substance use may actually further increase feelings of guilt and shame. Some questions you might use to explore the function of substance use with clients include:

> *Have you noticed that you have used alcohol or drugs as a way to cope with your feelings of guilt or shame? Does this work every time? The times it has not worked, how was that for you?*
>
> *Even if/when it does work to help you feel better, are there downsides to your substance use? What are they and how do they affect you? Your relationships? Your goals?*
>
> *What have been some of the benefits of using alcohol/drugs?*

If a client is abusing alcohol or other drugs, a concurrent treatment approach is recommended. This may mean the therapist is treating both the NAGS and the substance use, or it may mean the therapist is only treating the NAGS and the client is concurrently attending drug treatment. If the latter is true, we recommend the therapist communicates with other clinicians regarding the client's progress.

There are several circumstances in which a concurrent treatment approach may not be recommended. Engagement in TrIGR would not be recommended if the client is unable to present to sessions without having used substances, or if the client's substance use is interfering with their ability to engage in homework assignments. It is important to set some guidelines with the client so that their use does not interfere with their ability to benefit from TrIGR. If the client is not able to agree to not use prior to sessions or during or immediately following sessions or homework assignments, this may not be the right time to do TrIGR.

TrIGR may not be the most appropriate intervention if the client has a significant increase in their alcohol or substance use following therapy sessions. Under these circumstances, the recommendation would be to engage in substance use treatment prior to starting the TrIGR protocol. Using motivational interviewing may be especially helpful with this client. The therapist may want to encourage the client to seek additional support through mutual-help groups within the community such as Alcoholics Anonymous, Narcotics Anonymous, SMART Recovery and, if necessary, receive additional therapy that is focused on substance use disorders. Lastly, we encourage the therapist to spend some time each session checking in regarding use and cravings during the past week.

If the client is unwilling or unable to not let their use interfere with TrIGR, or the clinician is unfamiliar or uncomfortable working with clients who are abusing alcohol or drugs, referral to another provider may be appropriate.

Religious beliefs

Religion is often considered a tricky topic to delve into in therapy, but can be critical for some clients (Post & Wade, 2009). Many clients have religious or spiritual beliefs and want to discuss religious or spiritual issues in the context of therapy (Rose, Westefeld, & Ansley, 2008). Highly relevant to psychotherapy, many clients rely on spiritual and religious forms of coping, and this may be even more true for some groups (e.g., service members and Veterans (Department of Defense, 2013) and African American women (El-Khoury et al., 2004)). Additionally, a common correlate of posttraumatic distress is a weakening or loss of religious faith and for many this is a more compelling reason to seek treatment than their PTSD symptoms (Fontana & Rosenheck, 2004). Moral injury among Veterans can weaken or challenge spiritual and religious beliefs (Jinkerson, 2016). Also, many religions have explicit references to guilt and shame and prescribed practices to address them, some of which may actually reinforce guilt and shame (e.g., self-punishment). Fontana and Rosenheck (2004) found that among over 1300 Veterans, trauma-related guilt contributed to weakening of religious faith following combat trauma. In TriGR, we give clients the opportunity to consider and set goals around values having to do with spirituality and religion in Module 3. For some clients, religious beliefs may be a large contributor to making meaning of why the trauma occurred. Therapists can help clients explore such beliefs throughout TrIGR and can discuss with clients whether talking with a chaplain or religious leader may be helpful.

Clients who want to make amends or take reparative actions

Some of our clients believe that to move forward from their guilt and shame, they need to apologize to a victim of their trauma (e.g., a person they hurt, or the family member of someone who died during their trauma) or take reparative action (e.g., do something to make up for the victim's pain). Making amends or taking reparative action may help to alleviate guilt and shame but we recommend caution. A complicating factor for making amends is that it involves other people, making the outcome unpredictable. For example, attempting to repair damage to a relationship may not provide the desired relief if others involved do not want to repair the relationship.

In some religions, atonement, or penance, is considered a reparative behavior that can be prescribed in a time-limited way and is intended to be commensurate with the wrongdoing (Fisher & Exline, 2010). There are concerns, however, that engaging in reparative behavior prematurely, before honest evaluation of trauma-related guilt and shame, could serve to reinforce NAGS. Therefore, we recommend that clients who want to engage in some reparative behavior first complete a thorough guilt appraisal, review pros and cons of different actions they are considering, and make sure they recognize that while they can control what they do, they cannot control the outcome and it may not go the way they hope. Finally, it is important to consider the potential impact on the person who is the recipient of the reparative action. Might it in some way hurt or retraumatize the person? Such concerns should be discussed with clients and considered as clients formulate their plans.

Conclusion

One thing we have learned in our work is that there is no cookie cutter, standard relationship between certain types of traumas and NAGS. We can see 100 people with the same trauma type, such as combat or sexual assault, and hear 100 different reasons people feel guilt and shame. What we tried to do in this chapter is describe a few patterns we found so that you can keep an eye out for them when working with a client with these backgrounds. If you find any of the patterns we described to be true for your client, we hope the tips we provided are helpful. However, most important is to work with the person in the room with you, to get to know them, their trauma and their reasons for feeling guilt and shame. It is this understanding that will have the biggest role in determining if TrIGR is helpful to them.

PART 2 PREPARATION AND CASE RELATED CONSIDERATIONS

CHAPTER 8

Therapist self-care

Helping clients process traumatic events can be incredibly rewarding. Our clients share events with us that are deeply personal, and with trauma work, we are often the only person trusted with this information. Many mental health providers find the therapeutic relationship to be a great source of professional satisfaction. On the other hand, mental health providers, especially trauma therapists, are also at risk of compassion fatigue and burnout (Garcia et al., 2015). Even for the most seasoned therapist, repeated exposure to trauma details and/or feeling a sense of responsibility for clients can have a burdensome impact and can elicit very complex reactions. In extreme circumstances, therapists can experience vicarious traumatization or secondary traumatic stress symptoms, which can mimic PTSD symptoms (Figley, 1995; McCann & Pearlman, 1990). Unchecked, burnout can lead to lower work satisfaction, increased absenteeism and lateness, decreased effectiveness and productivity, and leaving clinical work altogether (Pearlman & Saakvitne, 1995).

We would love it if this chapter were unnecessary. However, we know firsthand how difficult it can be to "bear witness" to the trauma stories that clients share with us. Even when we are used to working with trauma, something about a particular trauma can hit us hard or we can start to feel burned out in general. We, therefore, decided to include this chapter as a reminder of the importance of checking in with, and intentionally taking care of, yourself. Below, we review risk factors and warning signs of burnout and share strategies for preventing compassion fatigue or changing course if signs are already present. For readers who would like more in-depth guidance for practicing self-care beyond what we cover in this chapter, there are several comprehensive resources that may be helpful (e.g., Wicks & Maynard, 2014).

Trauma Informed Guilt Reduction Therapy
https://doi.org/10.1016/B978-0-12-814780-1.00008-3

Risks of burnout

The following are the risk factors for burnout. Research studies have found that people who work under these conditions are more likely to experience burnout than others (Adams, Boscarino, & Figley, 2006; Arvay, 2001; Benson & Magraith, 2005; Craig & Sprang, 2010; Creamer & Liddle, 2005).

(1) Heavy caseload

(2) Long work days

(3) Insufficient resources to meet your client's needs (e.g., lack of materials, not enough availability of case management)

(4) Insufficient resources to meet your own needs (e.g., limited training opportunities, no consultation available)

(5) Difficult working environment (e.g., lack of support from colleagues and supervisors, limited opportunities for growth, inconsistent procedures/policies)

(6) Not able to use vacation days

Signs of burnout

Experiencing the following emotional, physical, or behavioral signs often and intensely, especially in relation to work, may be signs of burnout (Maslach, 1993; Fothergill, Edwards, & Burnard, 2004).

Emotional signs

Decreased compassion and empathy; emotional exhaustion; emotional numbing; cynicism; boredom; irritability; depression/hopelessness; anxiety/confusion; and voyeuristic tendencies with regard to clients.

Physical signs

Headaches; muscle aches/tension/twitches; gastrointestinal distress; heart palpitations; changes in appetite: overeating/weight gain or undereating/weight loss; memory difficulties; and frequent colds/illnesses.

Behavioral signs

Boundary rigidity (e.g., making distinctions between us vs. them); boundary violations (e.g., rescuing); distractions in session (e.g., checking watch and phone); calling off work or missing meetings; decreased productivity; being judgmental; isolation; insomnia/worry about work; and substance abuse.

Preventing and addressing burnout

When we recognize signs of burnout in ourselves, we have an opportunity to "practice what we preach," or in other words, to apply the helpful strategies we teach our clients to help ourselves. For example, you can practice relaxation strategies, reach out to your support system, take part in enjoyable activities, assess the effectiveness of your behaviors and accuracy of your thoughts, or seek additional training and/or consultation as needed. And of course, arrange for your own therapy if you find you are dealing with something more chronic and the above steps are not helping enough.

Phelps, Lloyd, Creamer, and Forbes (2009) proposed several practical steps to head off burnout or abate it once it starts. We have found these strategies helpful in our own work.

(1) *Engage in self-monitoring and self-reflection.* The goal is to notice signs of burnout early and intervene swiftly. Methods for practicing self-awareness and self-reflection that some find helpful are mindfulness or meditation. Such practice can increase your ability to engage in self-awareness during therapy sessions, and self-reflection in between sessions, so that you can monitor your own feelings, thoughts, and behaviors.

(2) *Seek support.* Seeking support and consultation from others is an excellent way to process your experience out loud and have a sounding board. While maintaining the confidentiality of your clients, share your success stories, and consult with your peers often on strenuous and difficult cases.

(3) *Maintain your boundaries.* Setting and maintaining healthy boundaries are important in every therapeutic relationship, but you may need to be more intentional about it in your work with clients who have experienced trauma. People experiencing posttraumatic distress may have limited support, feel helpless, and have a poor sense of self-competency. These reactions can contribute to some therapists feeling like they have to "rescue" their client or help them with all of their needs (e.g., allow for

extended appointments or excessive telephone access). If you find that you are working harder than your clients, this may be a time to reassess boundaries.

(4) *Know your limitations*. It will better serve you and your clients to acknowledge your limitations and set clear realistic expectations for therapy right from the start. While we should provide high quality care to all clients, and making accommodations to meet clients' particular needs is appropriate, trying to be *everything* to a client, to meet every request, every time, is not helpful to us or to them. Recognize and accept your own limitations related to your professional knowledge base and scope of practice, *and* your personal needs. Be willing to make referrals when needed.

(5) *Respect client autonomy*. This involves explicitly asserting that your client makes their own decisions and that they are responsible for their own choices and behaviors. Your role is to help your client make informed decisions and to develop a sense of independence and self-competence by providing them with information, assuming a supportive stance, and acknowledging their accomplishments over time.

(6) *Maintain physical and mental health*. Maintaining physical and mental health is vital to being an effective therapist as well as to circumventing burnout. In addition to the obvious strategies of eating healthy foods, exercising regularly, and having enough downtime and sleep, we encourage you to engage in activities that stimulate the emotional, intellectual, spiritual, and aesthetic facets of your being. Some therapists have found it helpful to take part in social change activities as a strategy that can help instill a sense of hope and empowerment which may counteract negative effects of being exposed to many traumatic stories (Harrison & Westwood, 2009; Iliffe & Steed, 2000).

PART 2 PREPARATION AND CASE RELATED CONSIDERATIONS

CHAPTER 9

TrIGR in a group format

Introduction

While the Trauma Informed Guilt Reduction (TrIGR) protocol was initially developed as an individual psychotherapy, it may also be provided in a group format. The group format allows a client to get input and feedback from other group members who have experienced similar traumatic events. The decision to deliver this therapy in individual vs group format should be guided by a number of factors, including the setting, resources, and therapist training and preferences. In this chapter, we discuss some of these considerations, describe how TrIGR's format and content can be adapted for group therapy, and provide suggestions of how to address some of the issues that are unique to delivering TrIGR in a group format. It is most useful to read this chapter after having read through the manual and workbook.

Preliminary considerations

Sometimes purely practical reasons are the catalyst for providing group therapy; for example, if there is not enough staffing or time to provide individual treatment to all the clients seeking services. But there may be other good reasons, such as giving clients the opportunity to see that others have had similar experiences and reactions, and to get feedback from peers.

Participating in a TrIGR group involves sharing details about traumatic events and related problems not just with the therapist but also with peers. For this reason, it may be best to compose the group of clients who have had similar traumatic experiences such as all combat Veterans or all interpersonal violence survivors. This can help clients feel more comfortable sharing their traumas with others and can allow them to draw from their own experiences when asking questions or providing feedback.

Trauma Informed Guilt Reduction Therapy
https://doi.org/10.1016/B978-0-12-814780-1.00009-5

One important aspect to consider is group size. In our clinical experience, we have found that beginning a TrIGR group with 8–10 clients is optimal. If possible, it is helpful for two co-therapists to lead the group in order to balance the presentation of didactic information with attention to group process and client reactions, especially when group members may be processing intense emotions. Finally, it can be useful to meet briefly with participants one-on-one prior to starting the group in order to cover information about confidentiality and group rules (these will be covered again during the first group meeting; see below for sample TrIGR group rules), assess readiness to address guilt and shame (see Chapter 6), have the client briefly describe the traumatic event, and provide an overview of TrIGR group format and content.

Overview of TrIGR group format

The same content is covered in TrIGR group format as in individual format (see Table 1). The group is typically conducted in weekly, 90-min sessions and generally takes more sessions to complete in group than individual format. In the group format, each client has a session focused on processing their trauma; therefore, the number of total sessions will depend on the number of participants. Therapists may also use clinical judgment and determine if time allows for adequate processing of two members' traumas during one group session.

Module 1. The beginning sessions, with the focus on providing psychoeducation about common reactions to traumatic events, common mental health problems, and learning about guilt are largely similar in group and individual formats. The group setting affords the opportunity for members to share with each other their experience with trauma-related symptoms and how these experiences have impacted their lives. These early group discussions are usually when clients start to see that others have had similar experiences with guilt and shame. The group also begins to build cohesion and a sense of safety and camaraderie.

Module 2. In individual therapy, clients learn how to take guilt apart and look at its components (hindsight bias, justification, responsibility analysis, etc.) at the same time as they process the trauma. However, in the group format, we have found it helpful to devote a session to teaching clients how to examine guilt events (i.e., debrief) before having a client apply the skills to their own trauma. Specifically, we have found that utilizing case vignettes that are relevant to the group's particular type of trauma is helpful to familiarize participants to the cognitive errors in a format that is less

Table 1 Sample overview of TrIGR group sessions

Session 1: Introductions, overview of TrIGR therapy, review of PTSD and other common symptoms and rationale for focus on guilt
Review group rules
PTSD and other common posttraumatic reactions
Why focus on guilt?
Session 2: Introduction to guilt and shame
Why do we experience guilt?
Why is guilt so complicated?
Common types of guilt
Introduce guilt cognitions log
Session 3: Introduction to guilt appraisal
Learn to take guilt apart
Use hypothetical examples to illustrate thinking patterns
Conduct responsibility and justification analyses
Sessions 4–9: Guilt debriefing of members' traumatic events
Members take turns sharing an account of their event and related guilt cognitions
Group leaders and members work together applying thinking patterns and conducting analyses; ask questions and provide feedback
Session 10: Identification of values
What are values and how are they affected by trauma?
Reconnecting with values
Session 11: Commitment to living a valued life
Review of goals worksheet
Steps to living a valued life
Planning how to achieve goals
Session 12: Termination (optional)
Review key points and feedback
Discuss reactions to group and collect feedback from members
Discuss plans to continue moving forward

emotionally charged than beginning with a group member's personal experience. Group members apply the debrief material to the vignettes as a group exercise, which mirrors the format of the next several sessions.

We then begin having group members take turns on consecutive weeks applying what they have learned to their own events, with group leaders and members asking questions and providing feedback. Group members are provided copies of worksheets to keep practicing each skill.

[**Therapist note:** *Anticipatory anxiety is high as clients prepare to discuss their traumatic event in a group setting. There are various ways to select the order in which participants share their experiences (e.g., asking for volunteers, drawing names out of a hat, etc.). We found it helpful to ask that all members be prepared to discuss their event each week and for the therapist(s) to select the particular member to share based on clinical judgment. We do not forecast our choice the week before; however, when there is only one group member left to share it will be obvious that their turn comes next.*]

Module 3. No specific modifications are made for delivering this content in a group format.

Additional considerations

While recording sessions is a part of the individual TrIGR protocol, we do not ask participants to do so in groups because of privacy issues. However, we suggest that clients record their own debriefing session (only their own) to listen to again following the session. This is optional and requires the consent of all the clients in the group. We have found that group members are frequently very anxious during the guilt appraisal and discussion, and are thus less able to retain key discussion points and feedback later on. Having access to an audio recording allows participants to review the feedback again in private when they are less anxious, which helps to reinforce what they learned. Most clients use their cell phone to record the session.

Similarly, it is often helpful to encourage participants to jot down two to three bullet points of the most useful or impactful feedback, or new and more accurate cognitions, to take away with them when the group ends. Finally, depending on available resources and the setting, therapists may consider offering a "booster session" spaced out 1 month or longer following the final group session. Reconvening the group is often useful in order to gauge continued progress toward non-avoidance, practicing new cognitions, and engaging in values-driven activities.

Sample TrIGR group rules template

TRAUMA INFORMED GUILT REDUCTION GROUP

[*Insert DATE, TIME, and LOCATION*]

GROUP LEADERS: [*Insert leaders' names and contact info*]

Group Rules and Expectations

1. All group members agree to respect the confidentiality of information they learn from others during the group. This means not discussing what is shared in group with others outside of group. You may talk outside the group about what you have learned or experienced yourself, but please do not discuss other group members or what they share in the group, even without using names.
2. The therapist(s) will respect your right to privacy and confidentiality. However, the legal limits to confidentiality include:
   - If you state that you wish and plan to harm yourself or anyone else, we must report this to people outside the group and take action to ensure your safety and the safety of others.
   - If you indicate that you are or someone you know is harming *a child or* an elderly person [check state specific reporting laws and modify as needed], we must also report this to authorities to protect individuals' safety.
3. Group members are expected to behave in ways that will not be threatening, intimidating, or provoking to others in the group. All cell phones must be silenced or turned off during the group.
4. Group sessions will include discussion of traumatic events. If you feel you need to take a break from the group at any time you may do so but are expected to return to group prior to the end.
5. Group members are expected to attend meetings free of substances that could impair your ability to function in the group. Medications should be taken only as prescribed.
6. Members are expected to attend all sessions. Please call ______________
   ____
   [*Insert group leader's name and phone number*]. If you miss a session and are not able to call in advance, please call afterward so the group leaders are aware of how you are doing.

Emergency procedures: If you feel you are in crisis (i.e., suicidal or homicidal) and need immediate help, please call 911 or go to the nearest Hospital Emergency Room. At any time (24 hours a day, 7 days a week) you may contact the **Crisis Hotline: 1-800 273-TALK (8255).**

References

Abel, G. G. (1974). The role of fantasy in the treatment of sexual deviation. *Archives of General Psychiatry, 30*(4), 467–475. https://doi.org/10.1001/archpsyc.1974.01760100035007.

Adams, R. E., Boscarino, J. A., & Figley, C. R. (2006). Compassion fatigue and psychological distress among social workers: A validation study. *American Journal of Orthopsychiatry, 76*(1), 103–108. https://doi.org/10.1037/0002-9432.76.1.103.

American Psychiatric Association. (2013). *Diagnostic and statistical manual of mental disorders (DSM-5®)* (5th ed.). Arlington, VA: American Psychiatric Publishing.

Amstadter, A. B., & Vernon, L. L. (2008). Emotional reactions during and after trauma: A comparison of trauma types. *Journal of Aggression, Maltreatment & Trauma, 16*(4), 391–408. https://doi.org/10.1080/10926770801926492.

Arvay, M. J. (2001). Secondary traumatic stress among trauma counsellors: What does the research say? *International Journal for the Advancement of Counselling, 23*(4), 283–293. https://doi.org/10.1023/A:1014496419410.

Back, S. E., Foa, E. B., Kileen, T. K., Teeson, M., Dansky Cotton, B., & Carroll, K. M. (2015). *Concurrent treatment of PTSD and substance use disorders using prolonged exposure (COPE).* New York, NY: Oxford University Press.

Bass, J. K., Annan, J., McIvor Murray, S., Kaysen, D., Griffiths, S., Cetinoglu, T., … Bolton, P. A. (2013). Controlled trial of psychotherapy for Congolese survivors of sexual violence. *New England Journal of Medicine, 368*(23), 2182–2191. https://doi.org/10.1056/NEJMoa1211853.

Benson, J., & Magraith, K. (2005). Compassion fatigue and burnout: The role of Balint groups. *Australian Family Physician, 34*(6), 497–498.

Berman, A. H., Bergman, H., Palmstierna, T., & Schlyter, F. (2005). Evaluation of the Drug Use Disorders Identification Test (DUDIT) in criminal justice and detoxification settings and in a Swedish population sample. *European Addiction Research, 11*(1), 22–31. https://doi.org/10.1159/000081413.

Blake, D. D., Weathers, F. W., Nagy, L. M., Kaloupek, D. G., Gusman, F. D., Charney, D. S., & Keane, T. M. (1995). The development of a Clinician-Administered PTSD Scale. *Journal of Traumatic Stress, 8*(1), 75–90. https://doi.org/10.1007/BF02105408.

Blum, A. (2008). Shame and guilt, misconceptions and controversies: A critical review of the literature. *Traumatology, 14*(3), 91–102. https://doi.org/10.1177/1534765608321070.

Bovin, M. J., Black, S. K., Rodriguez, P., Lunney, C. A., Kleiman, S. E., Weathers, F. W., … Marx, B. P. (2018). Development and validation of a measure of PTSD-related psychosocial functional impairment: The Inventory of Psychosocial Functioning. *Psychological Services, 15*(2), 216–229. https://doi.org/10.1037/ser0000220.

Breitenbecher, K. H. (2006). The relationships among self-blame, psychological distress, and sexual victimization. *Journal of Interpersonal Violence, 21*(5), 597–611. https://doi.org/10.1177/0886260506286842.

Briere, J., Smiljanich, K., & Henschel, D. (1994). Sexual fantasies, gender, and molestation history. *Child Abuse & Neglect, 18*(2), 131–137. https://doi.org/10.1016/0145-2134(94)90115-5.

Browne, K. C., Trim, R. S., Myers, U. S., & Norman, S. B. (2015). Trauma-related guilt: Conceptual development and relationship with posttraumatic stress and depressive symptoms. *Journal of Traumatic Stress, 28*(2), 134–141. https://doi.org/10.1002/jts.21999.

Bryan, C. J., Morrow, C. E., Etienne, N., & Ray-Sannerud, B. (2013a). Guilt, shame, and suicidal ideation in a military outpatient clinical sample. *Depression and Anxiety, 30*(1), 55–60. https://doi.org/10.1002/da.22002.

Bryan, C. J., Ray-Sannerud, B., Morrow, C. E., & Etienne, N. (2013b). Guilt is more strongly associated with suicidal ideation among military personnel with direct combat exposure. *Journal of Affective Disorders, 148*(1), 37–41. https://doi.org/10.1016/j.jad.2012.11.044.

Buchanan, M., Anderson, J. O., Uhlemann, M. R., & Horwitz, E. (2006). Secondary traumatic stress: An investigation of Canadian mental health workers. *Traumatology, 12*(4), 272–281. https://doi.org/10.1177/1534765606297817.

Burgess, A. W., & Holmstrom, L. L. (1976). Coping behavior of the rape victim. *American Journal of Psychiatry, 133*(4), 413–418.

Bush, K. (1998). The AUDIT Alcohol Consumption Questions (AUDIT-C): An effective brief screening test for problem drinking. *Archives of Internal Medicine, 158*(16), 1789. https://doi.org/10.1001/archinte.158.16.1789.

Cacciola, J. S., Alterman, A. I., DePhilippis, D., Drapkin, M. L., Valadez, C., Fala, N. C., … McKay, J. R. (2013). Development and initial evaluation of the Brief Addiction Monitor (BAM). *Journal of Substance Abuse Treatment, 44*(3), 256–263. https://doi.org/10.1016/j.jsat.2012.07.013.

Cahill, C., Llewelyn, S. P., & Pearson, C. (1991). Long-term effects of sexual abuse which occurred in childhood: A review. *British Journal of Clinical Psychology, 30*(2), 117–130. https://doi.org/10.1111/j.2044-8260.1991.tb00927.x.

Carlson, E. B., Furby, L., Armstrong, J., & Shlaes, J. (1997). A conceptual framework for the long-term psychological effects of traumatic childhood abuse. *Child Maltreatment, 2*(3), 272–295. https://doi.org/10.1177/1077559597002003009.

Carmassi, C., Bertelloni, C. A., Gesi, C., Conversano, C., Stratta, P., Massimetti, G., … Dell'Osso, L. (2017). New DSM-5 PTSD guilt and shame symptoms among Italian earthquake survivors: Impact on maladaptive behaviors. *Psychiatry Research, 251*, 142–147. https://doi.org/10.1016/j.psychres.2016.11.026.

Chard, K. M., Schumm, J. A., McIlvain, S. M., Bailey, G. W., & Parkinson, B. R. (2011). Exploring the efficacy of a residential treatment program incorporating cognitive processing therapy-cognitive for veterans with PTSD and traumatic brain injury. *Journal of Traumatic Stress, 24*(3), 347–351. https://doi.org/10.1002/jts.20644.

Coffey, P., Leitenberg, H., Henning, K., Turner, T., & Bennett, R. T. (1996). Mediators of the long-term impact of child sexual abuse: Perceived stigma, betrayal, powerlessness, and self-blame. *Child Abuse & Neglect, 20*(5), 447–455. https://doi.org/10.1016/0145-2134(96)00019-1.

Corrigan, P. (2004). How stigma interferes with mental health care. *American Psychologist, 59*(7), 614–625. https://doi.org/10.1037/0003-066X.59.7.614.

Craig, C. D., & Sprang, G. (2010). Compassion satisfaction, compassion fatigue, and burnout in a national sample of trauma treatment therapists. *Anxiety, Stress, & Coping, 23*(3), 319–339. https://doi.org/10.1080/10615800903085818.

Creamer, T. L., & Liddle, B. J. (2005). Secondary traumatic stress among disaster mental health workers responding to the September 11 attacks. *Journal of Traumatic Stress, 18*(1), 89–96. https://doi.org/10.1002/jts.20008.

Currier, J. M., Holland, J. M., Drescher, K., & Foy, D. (2015). Initial psychometric evaluation of the moral injury questionnaire-military version. *Clinical Psychology & Psychotherapy, 22*(1), 54–63. https://doi.org/10.1002/cpp.1866.

Davies, M. (2002). Male sexual assault victims: A selective review of the literature and implications for support services. *Aggression and Violent Behavior, 7*(3), 203–214. https://doi.org/10.1016/S1359-1789(00)00043-4.

Department of Defense. (2013). *2011 Department of Defense Health Related Behaviors Survey of active duty military personnel.* Retrieved from https://www.murray.senate.gov/public/_cache/files/889efd07-2475-40ee-b3b0-508947957a0f/final-2011-hrb-active-duty-survey-report.pdf.

Department of Veterans Affairs, & Department of Defense. (2017). *VA/DOD clinical practice guideline for the management of post-traumatic stress disorder and acute stress reactions.* Retrieved from https://www.healthquality.va.gov/guidelines/MH/ptsd/VADoDPTSDCPGFinal012418.pdf.

Dorais, M. (2002). *Don't tell: The sexual abuse of boys* (2nd ed.). Montreal, Quebec: McGill-Queen's Press.

Doty, J., & Doty, C. (2012). Command responsibility and accountability. *Military Review, 92*(1), 35–38.

Dwight-Johnson, M., Unutzer, J., Sherbourne, C., Tang, L., & Wells, K. B. (2001). Can quality improvement programs for depression in primary care address patient preferences for treatment? *Medical Care, 39*(9), 934–944.

Edwards, K. M., Turchik, J. A., Dardis, C. M., Reynolds, N., & Gidycz, C. A. (2011). Rape myths: History, individual and institutional-level presence, and implications for change. *Sex Roles, 65*(11–12), 761–773. https://doi.org/10.1007/s11199-011-9943-2.

El-Khoury, M. Y., Dutton, M. A., Goodman, L. A., Engel, L., Belamaric, R. J., & Murphy, M. (2004). Ethnic differences in battered women's formal help-seeking strategies: A focus on health, mental health, and spirituality. *Cultural Diversity and Ethnic Minority Psychology, 10*(4), 383–393. https://doi.org/10.1037/1099-9809.10.4.383.

Elwyn, G., Frosch, D., Thomson, R., Joseph-Williams, N., Lloyd, A., Kinnersley, P., … Barry, M. (2012). Shared decision making: A model for clinical practice. *Journal of General Internal Medicine, 27*(10), 1361–1367. https://doi.org/10.1007/s11606-012-2077-6.

Farnsworth, J. K., Drescher, K. D., Nieuwsma, J. A., Walser, R. B., & Currier, J. M. (2014). The role of moral emotions in military trauma: Implications for the study and treatment of moral injury. *Review of General Psychology, 18*(4), 249–262. https://doi.org/10.1037/gpr0000018.

Feiring, C., & Taska, L. S. (2005). The persistence of shame following sexual abuse: A longitudinal look at risk and recovery. *Child Maltreatment, 10*(4), 337–349. https://doi.org/10.1177/1077559505276686.

Figley, C. R. (1995). Compassion fatigue: Toward a new understanding of the costs of caring. In B. H. Stamm (Ed.), *Secondary traumatic stress: Self-care issues for clinicians, researchers, and educators* (pp. 3–28). Baltimore, MD: The Sidran Press.

Finkelhor, D. (1987). The trauma of child sexual abuse: Two models. *Journal of Interpersonal Violence, 2*(4), 348–366. https://doi.org/10.1177/088626058700200402.

Finkelhor, D., & Browne, A. (1985). The traumatic impact of child sexual abuse: A conceptualization. *American Journal of Orthopsychiatry, 55*(4), 530–541. https://doi.org/10.1111/j.1939-0025.1985.tb02703.x.

First, M. B., Williams, J. B. W., Karg, R. S., & Spitzer, R. L. (2015). *Structured clinical interview for DSM-5 disorders, clinician version (SCID-5-CV).* Arlington, VA: American Psychiatric Association.

Fisher, M. L., & Exline, J. J. (2010). Moving toward self-forgiveness: Removing barriers related to shame, guilt, and regret. *Social and Personality Psychology Compass, 4*(8), 548–558. https://doi.org/10.1111/j.1751-9004.2010.00276.x.

Foa, E. B., Steketee, G., & Rothbaum, B. O. (1989). Behavioral/cognitive conceptualizations of post-traumatic stress disorder. *Behavior Therapy, 20*(2), 155–176. https://doi.org/10.1016/S0005-7894(89)80067-X.

Foa, E. B., Yusko, D. A., McLean, C. P., Suvak, M. K., Bux, D. A., Oslin, D., … Volpicelli, J. (2013). Concurrent naltrexone and prolonged exposure therapy for patients with comorbid alcohol dependence and PTSD: A randomized clinical trial. *Journal of the American Medical Association, 310*(5), 488–495. https://doi.org/10.1001/jama.2013.8268.

Fontana, A., & Rosenheck, R. (2004). Trauma, change in strength of religious faith, and mental health service use among veterans treated for PTSD. *The Journal of Nervous and Mental Disease, 192*(9), 579–584. https://doi.org/10.1097/01.nmd.0000138224.17375.55.

Fortney, J. C., Unützer, J., Wrenn, G., Pyne, J. M., Smith, G. R., Schoenbaum, M., & Harbin, H. T. (2017). A tipping point for measurement-based care. *Psychiatric Services, 68*(2), 179–188. https://doi.org/10.1176/appi.ps.201500439.

Fothergill, A., Edwards, D., & Burnard, P. (2004). Stress, burnout, coping and stress management in psychiatrists: Findings from a systematic review. *International Journal of Social Psychiatry, 50*(1), 54–65.

Frankfurt, S., & Frazier, P. (2016). A review of research on moral injury in combat veterans. *Military Psychology, 28*(5), 318–330. https://doi.org/10.1037/mil0000132.

Frazier, P. A. (2000). The role of attributions and perceived control in recovery from rape. *Journal of Personal and Interpersonal Loss, 5*(2–3), 203–225. https://doi.org/10.1080/10811440008409753.

Galliano, G., Noble, L., Travis, L., & Puechl, C. (1993). Victim reactions during rape/sexual assault: A preliminary study of the immobility response and its correlates. *Journal of Interpersonal Violence*, 109–114. https://doi.org/10.1177/088626093008001008.

Garcia, H. A., McGeary, C. A., Finley, E. P., Ketchum, N. S., McGeary, D. D., & Peterson, A. L. (2015). Burnout among psychiatrists in the Veterans Health Administration. *Burnout Research, 2*(4), 108–114. https://doi.org/10.1016/j.burn.2015.10.001.

Gaudet, C. M., Sowers, K. M., Nugent, W. R., & Boriskin, J. A. (2016). A review of PTSD and shame in military veterans. *Journal of Human Behavior in the Social Environment, 26*(1), 56–68. https://doi.org/10.1080/10911359.2015.1059168.

Gautam, S., Gupta, I. D., Batra, L., Sharma, H., Khandelwal, R., & Pant, A. (1998). Psychiatric morbidity among victims of bomb blast. *Indian Journal of Psychiatry, 40*(1), 41–45.

Gilbert, P. (1997). The evolution of social attractiveness and its role in shame, humiliation, guilt and therapy. *Psychology and Psychotherapy: Theory, Research and Practice, 70*(2), 113–147. https://doi.org/10.1111/j.2044-8341.1997.tb01893.x.

Gilbert, P., & Andrews, B. (1998). *Shame: Interpersonal behavior, psychopathology, and culture*. New York, NY: Oxford University Press.

Hannan, C., Lambert, M. J., Harmon, C., Nielsen, S. L., Smart, D. W., Shimokawa, K., & Sutton, S. W. (2005). A lab test and algorithms for identifying clients at risk for treatment failure. *Journal of Clinical Psychology, 61*(2), 155–163. https://doi.org/10.1002/jclp.20108.

Harman, R., & Lee, D. (2010). The role of shame and self-critical thinking in the development and maintenance of current threat in post-traumatic stress disorder. *Clinical Psychology & Psychotherapy, 17*(1), 13–24. https://doi.org/10.1002/cpp.636.

Harrison, R. L., & Westwood, M. J. (2009). Preventing vicarious traumatization of mental health therapists: Identifying protective practices. *Psychotherapy: Theory, Research, Practice, Training, 46*, 203–219. https://doi.org/10.1037/a0016081.

Hatfield, D., McCullough, L., Frantz, S. H. B., & Krieger, K. (2009). Do we know when our clients get worse? An investigation of therapists' ability to detect negative client change. *Clinical Psychology & Psychotherapy, 17*(1), 25–32. https://doi.org/10.1002/cpp.656.

Hayes, S. C., Strosahl, K. D., & Wilson, K. G. (2016). *Acceptance and commitment therapy: The process and practice of mindful change* (2nd ed.). New York, NY: The Guilford Press.

Healy, J. M., Stewart, A. J., & Copeland, A. P. (1993). The role of self-blame in children's adjustment to parental separation. *Personality and Social Psychology Bulletin, 19*(3), 279–289. https://doi.org/10.1177/0146167293193004.

Held, P., Owens, G. P., & Anderson, S. E. (2015). The interrelationships among trauma-related guilt and shame, disengagement coping, and PTSD in a sample of treatment-seeking substance users. *Traumatology: An International Journal, 21*(4), 285–292. https://doi.org/10.1037/trm0000050.

Herman, J. L. (1992). *Trauma and recovery: The aftermath of violence from domestic abuse*. New York, NY: Basic Books.

Hettema, J., Steele, J., & Miller, W. R. (2005). Motivational interviewing. *Annual Review of Clinical Psychology*, *1*(1), 91–111. https://doi.org/10.1146/annurev.clinpsy.1.102803.143833.

Holmes, G. R., Offen, L., & Waller, G. (1997). See no evil, hear no evil, speak no evil: Why do relatively few male victims of childhood sexual abuse receive help for abuse-related issues in adulthood? *Clinical Psychology Review*, *17*(1), 69–88. https://doi.org/10.1016/S0272-7358(96)00047-5.

Hunter, J. A., Goodwin, D. W., & Wilson, R. J. (1993). Attributions of blame in child sexual abuse victims. *Journal of Child Sexual Abuse*, *1*(3), 75–89. https://doi.org/10.1300/J070v01n03_06.

Iliffe, G., & Steed, L. G. (2000). Exploring the counselor's experience of working with perpetrators and survivors of domestic violence. *Journal of Interpersonal Violence*, *15*(4), 393–412. https://doi.org/10.1177/088626000015004004.

Itzhaky, L., Avidor, S., & Solomon, Z. (2017). Long-term guilt and hostility underlying posttraumatic stress symptoms in war combatants and ex-prisoners of war. *Journal of Loss and Trauma*, *22*(3), 228–239. https://doi.org/10.1080/15325024.2017.1284491.

Jinkerson, J. D. (2016). Defining and assessing moral injury: A syndrome perspective. *Traumatology*, *22*(2), 122–130. https://doi.org/10.1037/trm0000069.

Jonzon, E., & Lindblad, F. (2004). Disclosure, reactions, and social support: Findings from a sample of adult victims of child sexual abuse. *Child Maltreatment*, *9*(2), 190–200. https://doi.org/10.1177/1077559504264263.

Kar, N. (2006). Psychosocial issues following a natural disaster in a developing country: A qualitative longitudinal observational study. *International Journal of Disaster Medicine*, *4*(4), 169–176. https://doi.org/10.1080/15031430701875551.

Karakurt, G., Smith, D., & Whiting, J. (2014). Impact of intimate partner violence on women's mental health. *Journal of Family Violence*, *29*(7), 693–702. https://doi.org/10.1007/s10896-014-9633-2.

Karlin, B. E., & Cross, G. (2014). From the laboratory to the therapy room: National dissemination and implementation of evidence-based psychotherapies in the U.S. Department of Veterans Affairs Health Care System. *American Psychologist*, *69*(1), 19–33. https://doi.org/10.1037/a0033888.

Kelly, R. J., Wood, J. J., Gonzalez, L. S., MacDonald, V., & Waterman, J. (2002). Effects of mother-son incest and positive perceptions of sexual abuse experiences on the psychosocial adjustment of clinic-referred men. *Child Abuse & Neglect*, *26*(4), 425–441. https://doi.org/10.1016/S0145-2134(02)00317-4.

Kessler, R. C. (1995). Posttraumatic stress disorder in the national comorbidity survey. *Archives of General Psychiatry*, *52*(12), 1048–1060. https://doi.org/10.1001/archpsyc.1995.03950240066012.

Khantzian, E. J. (1985). The self-medication hypothesis of addictive disorders: Focus on heroin and cocaine dependence. *The American Journal of Psychiatry*, *142*(11), 1259–1264. https://doi.org/10.1176/ajp.142.11.1259.

Kim, S., Thibodeau, R., & Jorgensen, R. S. (2011). Shame, guilt, and depressive symptoms: A meta-analytic review. *Psychological Bulletin*, *137*(1), 68–96.

Kroenke, K., & Spitzer, R. L. (2002). The PHQ-9: A new depression diagnostic and severity measure. *Psychiatric Annals*, *32*(9), 509–515. https://doi.org/10.3928/0048-5713-20020901-06.

Kubany, E. S. (1994). A cognitive model of guilt typology in combat-related PTSD. *Journal of Traumatic Stress*, 7(1), 3–19.

Kubany, E. S., Abueg, F. R., Owens, J. A., Brennan, J. M., Kaplan, A. S., & Watson, S. B. (1995). Initial examination of a multidimensional model of trauma-related guilt: Applications to combat veterans and battered women. *Journal of Psychopathology and Behavioral Assessment*, *17*(4), 353–376. https://doi.org/10.1007/BF02229056.

Kubany, E. S., Haynes, S. N., Abueg, F. R., Manke, F. P., Brennan, J. M., & Stahura, C. (1996). Development and validation of the Trauma-Related Guilt Inventory (TRGI). *Psychological Assessment*, *8*(4), 428–444. https://doi.org/10.1037/1040-3590.8.4.428.

Kubany, E. S., Hill, E. E., Owens, J. A., Iannce-Spencer, C., McCaig, M. A., Tremayne, K. J., et al. (2004). Cognitive trauma therapy for battered women with PTSD (CTT-BW). *Journal of Consulting and Clinical Psychology*, *72*(1), 3–18. https://doi.org/10.1037/0022-006X.72.1.3.

Kubany, E. S., & Manke, F. P. (1995). Cognitive therapy for trauma-related guilt: Conceptual bases and treatment outlines. *Cognitive and Behavioral Practice*, *2*(1), 27–61. https://doi.org/10.1016/S1077-7229(05)80004-5.

Kubany, E. S., & Ralston, T. C. (1998). Cognitive therapy for trauma-related guilt. In V. M. Follette & J. I. Rusek (Eds.), *Cognitive-behavioral therapies for trauma* (pp. 124–161). New York, NY: The Guilford Press.

Kubany, E. S., & Watson, S. B. (2003). Guilt: Elaboration of a multidemensional model. *Psychological Record*, *53*(1), 51–90.

Larsen, S. E., Fleming, C. J. E., & Resick, P. A. (2019). Residual symptoms following empirically supported treatment for PTSD. *Psychological Trauma: Theory, Research, Practice, and Policy*, *11*(2), 207–215. https://doi.org/10.1037/tra0000384.

Laugharne, R., & Priebe, S. (2006). Trust, choice and power in mental health. *Social Psychiatry and Psychiatric Epidemiology*, *41*(11), 843–852. https://doi.org/10.1007/s00127-006-0123-6.

Le, Q. A., Doctor, J. N., Zoellner, L. A., & Feeny, N. C. (2014). Cost-effectiveness of prolonged exposure therapy versus pharmacotherapy and treatment choice in posttraumatic stress disorder (the optimizing PTSD treatment trial): A doubly randomized preference trial. *The Journal of Clinical Psychiatry*, *75*(03), 222–230. https://doi.org/10.4088/JCP.13m08719.

Lerner, M. J., & Montada, L. (1998). An overview. In *Responses to Victimizations and Belief in a Just World*. (pp. 1–7) Boston, MA: Springer. https://doi.org/10.1007/978-1-4757-6418-5_1.

Levin, R. J., & van Berlo, W. (2004). Sexual arousal and orgasm in subjects who experience forced or non-consensual sexual stimulation—a review. *Journal of Clinical Forensic Medicine*, *11*(2), 82–88. https://doi.org/10.1016/j.jcfm.2003.10.008.

Lewis, H. B. (1971). Shame and guilt in neurosis. *Psychoanalytic Review*, *58*(3), 419–438.

Litz, B. T., Stein, N., Delaney, E., Lebowitz, L., Nash, W. P., Silva, C., et al. (2009). Moral injury and moral repair in war veterans: A preliminary model and intervention strategy. *Clinical Psychology Review*, *29*(8), 695–706. https://doi.org/10.1016/j.cpr.2009.07.003.

Malloy, L. C., Lyon, T. D., & Quas, J. A. (2007). Filial dependency and recantation of child sexual abuse allegations. *Journal of the American Academy of Child & Adolescent Psychiatry*, *46*(2), 162–170. https://doi.org/10.1097/01.chi.0000246067.77953.f7.

Martin, G., & Pear, J. (1999). *Behavior modification: What it is and how to do it*. New York, NY: Prentice Hall.

Marx, B. P., Foley, K. M., Feinstein, B. A., Wolf, E. J., Kaloupek, D. G., & Keane, T. M. (2010). Combat-related guilt mediates the relations between exposure to combat-related abusive violence and psychiatric diagnoses. *Depression and Anxiety*, *27*(3), 287–293. https://doi.org/10.1002/da.20659.

Maslach, C. (1993). Burnout: A multidimensional perspective. In W. B. Schaufeli, C. Maslach, & T. Marek (Eds.), *Professional burnout* (pp. 19–32). Washington, DC: Taylor & Francis.

McCann, I. L., & Pearlman, L. A. (1990). Vicarious traumatization: A framework for understanding the psychological effects of working with victims. *Journal of Traumatic Stress*, *3*(1), 131–149. https://doi.org/10.1007/BF00975140.

Messman-Moore, T. L., & Coates, A. A. (2007). The impact of childhood psychological abuse on adult interpersonal conflict: The role of early maladaptive schemas and patterns of interpersonal behavior. *Journal of Emotional Abuse*, *7*(2), 75–92. https://doi.org/10.1300/J135v07n02_05.

Michalopoulos, L. T. M., Murray, L. K., Kane, J. C., van Wyk, S. S., Chomba, E., Cohen, J., … Bolton, P. A. (2015). Testing the validity and reliability of the shame questionnaire among sexually abused girls in Zambia. *PLoS One*, *10*(4), e0123820. https://doi.org/10.1371/journal.pone.0123820.

Miller, W. R., & Rollnick, S. (2013). *Motivational interviewing: Helping people change*. New York, NY: Guilford press.

Mittal, D., Drummond, K. L., Blevins, D., Curran, G., Corrigan, P., & Sullivan, G. (2013). Stigma associated with PTSD: Perceptions of treatment seeking combat veterans. *Psychiatric Rehabilitation Journal, 36*(2), 86–92. https://doi.org/10.1037/h0094976.

Moran, P. M., Bifulco, A., Ball, C., Jacobs, C., & Benaim, K. (2002). Exploring psychological abuse in childhood: I. Developing a new interview scale. *Bulletin of the Menninger Clinic, 66*(3), 213–240. https://doi.org/10.1521/bumc.66.3.213.23367.

Murdoch, M., Pryor, J. B., Polusny, M. A., & Gackstetter, G. D. (2007). Functioning and psychiatric symptoms among military men and women exposed to sexual stressors. *Military Medicine, 172*(7), 718–725. https://doi.org/10.7205/MILMED.172.7.718.

Murphy, R. T., Thompson, K. E., Murray, M., Rainey, Q., & Uddo, M. M. (2009). Effect of a motivation enhancement intervention on veterans' engagement in PTSD treatment. *Psychological Services, 6*(4), 264–278. https://doi.org/10.1037/a0017577.

Murray, L. K., Familiar, I., Skavenski, S., Jere, E., Cohen, J., Imasiku, M., … Bolton, P. (2013). An evaluation of trauma focused cognitive behavioral therapy for children in Zambia. *Child Abuse & Neglect, 37*(12), 1175–1185. https://doi.org/10.1016/j.chiabu.2013.04.017.

Nash, W. P., Marino Carper, T. L., Mills, M. A., Au, T., Goldsmith, A., & Litz, B. T. (2013). Psychometric evaluation of the moral injury events scale. *Military Medicine, 178*(6), 646–652. https://doi.org/10.7205/MILMED-D-13-00017.

Nelson, K. G., Young, K., & Chapman, H. (2014). Examining the performance of the brief addiction monitor. *Journal of Substance Abuse Treatment, 46*(4), 472–481. https://doi.org/10.1016/j.jsat.2013.07.002.

Norman, S. B., Haller, M., Kim, H. M., Allard, C. B., Porter, K. E., Stein, M. B., et al. (2018). Trauma related guilt cognitions partially mediate the relationship between PTSD symptom severity and functioning among returning combat veterans. *Journal of Psychiatric Research, 100*, 56–62. https://doi.org/10.1016/j.jpsychires.2018.02.003.

Norman, S. B., & Hamblen, J. L. (2017). Promising directions for treating comorbid PTSD and substance use disorder. *Alcoholism: Clinical and Experimental Research, 41*(4), 708–710. https://doi.org/10.1111/acer.13349.

Norman, S. B., Wilkins, K. C., Myers, U. S., & Allard, C. B. (2014). Trauma informed guilt reduction therapy with combat veterans. *Cognitive and Behavioral Practice, 21*(1), 78–88. https://doi.org/10.1016/j.cbpra.2013.08.001.

O'Connor, A. M., Wennberg, J. E., Legare, F., Llewellyn-Thomas, H. A., Moulton, B. W., Sepucha, K. R., et al. (2007). Toward the 'Tipping Point': Decision aids and informed patient choice. *Health Affairs, 26*(3), 716–725. https://doi.org/10.1377/hlthaff.26.3.716.

Øktedalen, T., Hagtvet, K. A., Hoffart, A., Langkaas, T. F., & Smucker, M. (2014). The trauma related shame inventory: Measuring trauma-related shame among patients with PTSD. *Journal of Psychopathology and Behavioral Assessment, 36*(4), 600–615. https://doi.org/10.1007/s10862-014-9422-5.

Opp, R. E., & Samson, A. Y. (1989). Taxonomy of guilt for combat veterans. *Professional Psychology: Research and Practice, 20*(3), 159–165.

Orsillo, S. M., & Batten, S. V. (2005). Acceptance and commitment therapy in the treatment of posttraumatic stress disorder. *Behavior Modification, 29*(1), 95–129.

Owens, G. P., Chard, K. M., & Ann Cox, T. (2008). The relationship between maladaptive cognitions, anger expression, and posttraumatic stress disorder among veterans in residential treatment. *Journal of Aggression, Maltreatment & Trauma, 17*(4), 439–452. https://doi.org/10.1080/10926770802473908.

Pearlman, L. A., & Mac Ian, P. S. (1995). Vicarious traumatization: An empirical study of the effects of trauma work on trauma therapists. *Professional Psychology: Research and Practice, 26*(6), 558–565. https://doi.org/10.1037/0735-7028.26.6.558.

Pearlman, L. A., & Saakvitne, K. W. (1995). *Trauma and the therapist: Countertransference and vicarious traumatization in psychotherapy with incest survivors*. New York, NY: WW Norton & Co.

Persons, J. B. (2012). *The case formulation approach to cognitive-behavior therapy*. New York, NY: Guilford Press.

Petrakis, I. L., & Simpson, T. L. (2017). Posttraumatic stress disorder and alcohol use disorder: A critical review of pharmacologic treatments. *Alcoholism: Clinical and Experimental Research*, *41*(2), 226–237. https://doi.org/10.1111/acer.13297.

Phelps, A., Lloyd, D., Creamer, M., & Forbes, D. (2009). Caring for carers in the aftermath of trauma. *Journal of Aggression, Maltreatment & Trauma*, *18*(3), 313–330. https://doi.org/10.1080/10926770902835899.

Pitman, A. L., Osborn, D. P. J., Rantell, K., & King, M. B. (2016). The stigma perceived by people bereaved by suicide and other sudden deaths: A cross-sectional UK study of 3432 bereaved adults. *Journal of Psychosomatic Research*, *87*, 22–29. https://doi.org/10.1016/j.jpsychores.2016.05.009.

Posner, K., Brent, D., Lucas, C., Gould, M., Stanley, B., Brown, G., et al. (2008). *Columbia-suicide severity rating scale (C-SSRS)*. New York, NY: The Research Foundation for Mental Hygene.

Post, B. C., & Wade, N. G. (2009). Religion and spirituality in psychotherapy: A practice-friendly review of research. *Journal of Clinical Psychology*, *65*(2), 131–146. https://doi.org/10.1002/jclp.20563.

Pugh, L. R., Taylor, P. J., & Berry, K. (2015). The role of guilt in the development of post-traumatic stress disorder: A systematic review. *Journal of Affective Disorders*, *182*(Supplement C), 138–150. https://doi.org/10.1016/j.jad.2015.04.026.

Reinert, D. F., & Allen, J. P. (2002). The Alcohol Use Disorders Identification Test (AUDIT): A review of recent research. *Alcoholism: Clinical and Experimental Research*, *26*(2), 272–279. https://doi.org/10.1111/j.1530-0277.2002.tb02534.x.

Resick, P. A., Nishith, P., Weaver, T. L., Astin, M. C., & Feuer, C. A. (2002). A comparison of cognitive-processing therapy with prolonged exposure and a waiting condition for the treatment of chronic posttraumatic stress disorder in female rape victims. *Journal of Consulting and Clinical Psychology*, *70*(4), 867–879. https://doi.org/10.1037/0022-006X.70.4.867.

Rizvi, S. L., Kayen, D. J., Gutner, C. A., Griffin, M. G., & Resick, P. A. (2008). Beyond fear: The role of peritraumatic responses in posttraumatic stress and depressive symptoms among female crime victims. *Journal of Interpersonal Violence*, *23*(6), 853–868. https://doi.org/10.1177/0886260508314851.

Rokke, P. D., Tomhave, J. A., & Jocic, Z. (1999). The role of client choice and target selection in self-management therapy for depression in older adults. *Psychology and Aging*, *14*(1), 155–169. https://doi.org/10.1037/0882-7974.14.1.155.

Romano, E., & De Luca, R. V. (2001). Male sexual abuse: A review of effects, abuse characteristics, and links with later psychological functioning. *Aggression and Violent Behavior*, *6*(1), 55–78. https://doi.org/10.1016/S1359-1789(99)00011-7.

Rose, E. M., Westefeld, J. S., & Ansley, T. N. (2008). Spiritual issues in counseling: Clients' beliefs and preferences. *Psychology of Religion and Spirituality*, *S*(1), 18–33. https://doi.org/10.1037/1941-1022.S.1.18.

Rothschild, B., & Rand, M. (2006). *Help for the helper: Self-care strategies for managing burnout and stress*. New York & London: WW Norton & Company.

Rubak, S., Sandbaek, A., Lauritzen, T., & Christensen, B. (2005). Motivational interviewing: A systematic review and meta-analysis. *The British Journal of General Practice: The Journal of the Royal College of General Practitioners*, *55*(513), 305–312.

Saraiya, T., & Lopez-Castro, T. (2016). Ashamed and afraid: A scoping review of the role of shame in post-traumatic stress disorder (PTSD). *Journal of Clinical Medicine*, *5*(11), E94. https://doi.org/10.3390/jcm5110094.

Saunders, J. B., Aasland, O. G., Babor, T. F., De La Fuente, J. R., & Grant, M. (1993). Development of the Alcohol Use Disorders Identification Test (AUDIT): WHO collaborative project on early detection of persons with harmful alcohol consumption-II. *Addiction*, *88*(6), 791–804. https://doi.org/10.1111/j.1360-0443.1993.tb02093.x.

Schauben, L. J., & Frazier, P. A. (1995). Vicarious trauma: The effects on female counselors of working with sexual violence survivors. *Psychology of Women Quarterly*, *19*(1), 49–64. https://doi.org/10.1111/j.1471-6402.1995.tb00278.x.

Scheffer Lindgren, M., & Renck, B. (2008). 'It is still so deep-seated, the fear': Psychological stress reactions as consequences of intimate partner violence. *Journal of Psychiatric and Mental Health Nursing*, *15*(3), 219–228. https://doi.org/10.1111/j.1365-2850.2007.01215.x.

Seal, K. H., Abadjian, L., McCamish, N., Shi, Y., Tarasovsky, G., & Weingardt, K. (2012). A randomized controlled trial of telephone motivational interviewing to enhance mental health treatment engagement in Iraq and Afghanistan veterans. *General Hospital Psychiatry*, *34*(5), 450–459. https://doi.org/10.1016/j.genhosppsych.2012.04.007.

Sexton, L. (1999). Vicarious traumatisation of counsellors and effects on their workplaces. *British Journal of Guidance & Counselling*, *27*(3), 393–403. https://doi.org/10.1080/03069889908256279.

Simpson, T. L., Lehavot, K., & Petrakis, I. L. (2017). No wrong doors: Findings from a critical review of behavioral randomized clinical trials for individuals with co-occurring alcohol/drug problems and posttraumatic stress disorder. *Alcoholism: Clinical and Experimental Research*, *41*(4), 681–702. https://doi.org/10.1111/acer.13325.

Smith, D. W., Letourneau, E. J., Saunders, B. E., Kilpatrick, D. G., Resnick, H. S., & Best, C. L. (2000). Delay in disclosure of childhood rape: Results from a national survey. *Child Abuse & Neglect*, *24*(2), 273–287. https://doi.org/10.1016/S0145-2134(99)00130-1.

Smith, P. L., & Moss, S. B. (2009). Psychologist impairment: What is it, how can it be prevented, and what can be done to address it? *Clinical Psychology: Science and Practice*, *16*(1), 1–15. https://doi.org/10.1111/j.1468-2850.2009.01137.x.

Somasundaram, D. (2010). Collective trauma in the Vanni—a qualitative inquiry into the mental health of the internally displaced due to the civil war in Sri Lanka. *International Journal of Mental Health Systems*, *4*, 22. https://doi.org/10.1186/1752-4458-4-22.

Stotz, S. J., Elbert, T., Müller, V., & Schauer, M. (2015). The relationship between trauma, shame, and guilt: Findings from a community-based study of refugee minors in Germany. *European Journal of Psychotraumatology*, *6*(1), 25863. https://doi.org/10.3402/ejpt.v6.25863.

Street, A. E., & Arias, I. (2001). Psychological abuse and posttraumatic stress disorder in battered women: Examining the roles of shame and guilt. *Violence and Victims*, *16*(1), 65–78. https://doi.org/10.1891/0886-6708.16.1.65.

Street, A. E., Gibson, L. E., & Holohan, D. R. (2005). Impact of childhood traumatic events, trauma-related guilt, and avoidant coping strategies on PTSD symptoms in female survivors of domestic violence. *Journal of Traumatic Stress*, *18*(3), 245–252. https://doi.org/10.1002/jts.20026.

TalYoung, I., Iglewicz, A., Glorioso, D., Lanouette, N., Seay, K., Ilapakurti, M., & Zisook, S. (2012). Suicide bereavement and complicated grief. *Dialogues in Clinical Neuroscience*, *14*(2), 177–186.

Tang, S. S., Freyd, J. J., & Wang, M. (2008). What do we know about gender in the disclosure of child sexual abuse? *Journal of Psychological Trauma*, *6*(4), 1–26. https://doi.org/10.1080/19322880802096442.

Tangey, J., & Dearing, R. L. (2002). *Shame and guilt. Emotions and social behavior.* New York, NY: The Guilford Press.

Tangney, J. P. (1996). Conceptual and methodological issues in the assessment of shame and guilt. *Behaviour Research and Therapy*, *34*(9), 741–754. https://doi.org/10.1016/0005-7967(96)00034-4.

Tiwari, A., Wong, J., Brownridge, D. A., Chan, K. L., Fong, D. Y. T., Leung, W. C., et al. (2009). Psychological intimate partner abuse among Chinese women: What we know and what we still need to know. *The Open Social Science Journal*, *2*(1), 32–36. https://doi.org/10.2174/1874945300902010032.

Trinh, N.-H.T., Nadler, D. L., Shie, V., Fregni, F., Gilman, S. E., Ryan, C. M., & Schneider, J. C. (2014). Psychological sequelae of the station nightclub fire: Comparing survivors with and without physical injuries using a mixed-methods analysis. *PLoS One, 9*(12), e115013. https://doi.org/10.1371/journal.pone.0115013.

Tripp, J. C., & McDevitt-Murphy, M. E. (2017). Trauma-related guilt mediates the relationship between posttraumatic stress disorder and suicidal ideation in OEF/OIF/OND veterans. *Suicide and Life-threatening Behavior, 47*(1), 78–85. https://doi.org/10.1111/sltb.12266.

Ullman, D. S. E. (2007). Relationship to perpetrator, disclosure, social reactions, and PTSD symptoms in child sexual abuse survivors. *Journal of Child Sexual Abuse, 16*(1), 19–36. https://doi.org/10.1300/J070v16n01_02.

Ullman, S. E. (2002). Social reactions to child sexual abuse disclosures: A critical review. *Journal of Child Sexual Abuse, 12*(1), 89–121. https://doi.org/10.1300/J070v12n01_05.

Weathers, F. W., Litz, B. T., Keane, T. M., Palmieri, P. A., Marx, B. P., & Schnurr, P. P. (2013). *The PTSD Checklist for DSM5 (PCL-5)*. Scale Available from the National Center for PTSD at www.ptsd.va.gov.

Weaver, T. L., & Clum, G. A. (1995). Psychological distress associated with interpersonal violence: A meta-analysis. *Clinical Psychology Review, 15*(2), 115–140. https://doi.org/10.1016/0272-7358(95)00004-9.

Westerlund, E. (1992). *Women's sexuality after childhood incest*. New York: W.W. Norton. Retrieved from http://www.worldcat.org/title/womens-sexuality-after-childhood-incest/oclc/25508936.

Wicks, R. J., & Maynard, E. A. (2014). *Clinician's guide to self-renewal: Essential advice from the field*. Hoboken, New Jersey: John Wiley & Sons.

Wilkins, K. C., Lang, A. J., & Norman, S. B. (2011). Synthesis of the psychometric properties of the PTSD checklist (PCL) military, civilian, and specific versions. *Depression and Anxiety, 28*(7), 596–606. https://doi.org/10.1002/da.20837.

Wilkins, K. C., Myers, U. S., Goldsmith, A. A., Buzzella, B., & Norman, S. B. (2013). *High-risk behaviors in Iraq and Afghanistan veterans: The role of trauma-related guilt*. Presented at the Anxiety and Depression Association of America Annual Conference, La Jolla, CA.

Wilson, J. E., & Wilson, K. M. (2008). Amelioration of sexual fantasies to sexual abuse cues in an adult survivor of childhood sexual abuse: A case study. *Journal of Behavior Therapy and Experimental Psychiatry, 39*(4), 417–423. https://doi.org/10.1016/j.jbtep.2008.01.002.

Wilson, J. P., Droždek, B., & Turkovic, S. (2006). Posttraumatic shame and guilt. *Trauma, Violence, & Abuse, 7*(2), 122–141. https://doi.org/10.1177/1524838005285914.

World Health Organization. (1992). *The ICD-10 classification of mental and behavioural disorders: Clinical descriptions and diagnostic guidelines, Vol. 1*. World Health Organization.

World Health Organization. (1998). Development of the World Health Organization WHOQOL-BREF quality of life assessment. *Psychological Medicine, 28*(3), 551–558.

Yi, J. (2004). MCMAP and the marine warrior ethos. *Military Review, 17*(1), 17–24.

Yuen-Tsang, A., & Sung, P. (2005). The social construction of concealment among Chinese women in abusive marriages in Hong Kong. *Affilia, 20*(3), 284–299. https://doi.org/10.1177/0886109905277614.

PART 3

Therapist manual

MODULE 1, SESSIONS 1 AND 2

Introduction to posttraumatic guilt and shame

Introduction

The primary goal of Trauma Informed Guilt Reduction (TrIGR) therapy is to help clients reduce guilt and shame and the related distress that stems from traumatic events.

This manual walks the therapist through the three modules of the therapy, moving from psychoeducation, to debriefing the trauma and the accompanying guilt and shame cognitions, and, finally, to understanding how guilt can point to deeply held values and helping the client shift toward a future-oriented values-driven perspective. It is written as a script the therapist can use as a guide when presenting the content of each session. Therapists are strongly encouraged to learn the material prior to each session rather than read the manual verbatim to the client. Notes to the therapist that are not meant to be shared directly with the client are ***[bracketed, bolded, and italicized]***.

Please note that we have included scripts and examples that will apply to specific kinds of traumas (e.g., sexual trauma, military and first responder trauma, and suicide of a loved one) so that the therapist can draw from those that are most relevant to their particular clients. However, the therapist may include any examples as the information and processes apply to all types of trauma and it can sometimes be helpful for clients to hear examples that are different enough from their own in order to digest the information while feeling relatively less distress. In addition, we recommend that the therapist elicits examples from the client and uses them frequently throughout the treatment.

This manual is meant to guide the therapist through the process of treatment while the therapist individualizes the teaching style and examples to make the material relevant and understandable to the client. Therapeutic alliance is essential to any successful intervention and, in our experience, TrIGR promotes a strong alliance.

This manual should be used in conjunction with the TrIGR Client Workbook. Both the client and therapist should have a copy of the workbook to refer during each session. Prior to the first TrIGR session, make a copy of the entire workbook (included at the

Trauma Informed Guilt Reduction Therapy
https://doi.org/10.1016/B978-0-12-814780-1.09985-8

end of this book) for the client to use and refer to throughout the therapy. The client will be asked to complete the homework in the workbook as well.

The following are some additional tips to keep in mind as you start using TrIGR. Throughout the therapy, therapists should take note of: (1) guilt and shame talk so they can help the client recognize their guilt and shame cognitions, and (2) values talk to help the client identify the values that are important to them. The therapist should help the client get in the habit of writing guilt cognitions down on the Guilt and Shame Cognitions Log. With regard to identifying values talk, the therapist can bring these to the attention of the client by making statements such as, "It sounds like being there for your family is an important value for you." This will be especially relevant in Module 3.

Session 1: Overview of TrIGR, Introduction to Guilt and Shame

Session Agenda:
1. Introduce TrIGR format and content
2. Help the client understand guilt and its association with posttraumatic distress
3. Present psychoeducation about guilt and shame and why we experience them
4. Assign homework
5. Close the session

1. Introduce TrIGR format and content

What can you expect from this treatment program?

We will spend approximately 4–7 sessions focusing on the aspects of your trauma that still bother you; specifically, events about which you feel guilt and/or shame. By this, I mean events or experiences where you feel bad that you did not do something differently or react differently. It may be something that causes you a great deal of regret, something you beat yourself up about or something that is so painful to think about that you avoid doing so. It may be something that led you to conclude that you are a bad person, that there is something wrong with you, or that you somehow deserve to experience pain.

We will meet for up to 90 min each session and there will be practice assignments in between sessions. I will ask that you listen to a recording of each meeting at least once between sessions because we go over a lot of information and this will give you an extra way to process the information presented.

[Ask client to record session on cell phone or recording devise. Let client know you will ask them to listen to the session at least one time before the next meeting.]

[We have used 50–90 min sessions to conduct TrIGR. It is possible to use only 50 min sessions but it will likely take at least two sessions to get through Module 2.]

Over the course of treatment, we will focus on understanding why feelings of guilt and shame can be so painful after trauma, we will work to understand your particular situation, and we will look at what function guilt may be playing in your life. Feeling guilt or shame often means that you believe you have violated a value that is important to you. We will look at how guilt and shame are affecting you now, to better understand what you can do now to express those values in ways that feel meaningful to you.

The topics we will cover in TrIGR are:

1. Module 1: Introduction to posttraumatic guilt and shame
   a. Overview of TrIGR, introduction to guilt and shame
   b. Common problems and types of guilt related to trauma
2. Module 2: Debriefing the traumatic event and appraising trauma-related guilt and shame
   a. Guilt and shame appraisal
3. Module 3: Commitment to living a value-driven life and setting value-driven goals
   a. Commitment to living a value-driven life and setting value-driven goals
   b. A plan to live a valued life

Session Format

Each time we meet, I will share information that may help you understand your experiences, introduce new skills and the reasons we believe they may be helpful to you, and then we will practice these skills together.

We will then discuss the practice assignment that you will complete outside of the therapy sessions. For any skill to be effective, practice is necessary and this therapy is no different.

Finally, I will ask for your feedback. That is, what you learned, what you thought was helpful, and whether you have any questions or concerns.

During the first session, today, I will be talking quite a bit. I have a lot of important information to share and will also ask about your experiences. Please feel free to let me know if you have any questions or concerns about anything at any time. Also, I encourage you to take notes in your workbook as we go along.

Do you have any questions or concerns so far?

Introduce the Workbook

This is your workbook. It includes some readings to complement what we will be talking about in sessions, and worksheets for your practice assignments. Please write in it, take notes, write questions you want to bring up at our next session, etc. Use it, however it works best for you. Please remember to bring it to each session.

Are you ready to get started? Any questions before we begin?

2. Understanding guilt and shame and its relationship to trauma

The following are extremely common experiences following a traumatic event:

- Guilt: Feeling distress because you think you should have thought, felt, or acted differently.
- Shame: Feeling distress because you believe you are a bad person because of how you acted or reacted during the trauma.
- Anger: Distress because you think you or someone else should have thought, felt, or acted differently.
- Loss/Grief: Distress due to tangible losses such as the loss of friends or loved ones, belongings, career, and/or symbolic losses such as the loss of identity, innocence, self-worth, faith in God or human nature, optimism, or loss of control and loss of values and meaning.

Which of these can you relate to?

Tell me about how these experiences are affecting you right now?

Why focus on guilt?

Guilt is a frequent source of distress and pain following trauma.

[Choose the most relevant examples below that pertain to the particular client's experiences. Check in often with the client to make sure they grasp the information and ask if/how what you are saying relates to their experiences.]

Guilt and shame are common after just about all types of trauma. A car accident survivor may feel guilty that someone else was hurt. A domestic violence survivor may feel guilty for having stayed in the relationship or allowing children to witness the abuse. A sexual assault survivor may feel guilty for not having been able to stop the assault. Military service members may feel guilt based on having to do things, see things, and make decisions that have life and death consequences, and/or being unable to stop things that go against their core values (like not hurting others, standing up for themselves or their integrity, honor, courage, and protecting others).

You may develop a sense of having gone so far against your values that it feels like you will never see yourself, others, or the world in the same way again. In this therapy, we refer to this as trauma-related guilt and shame. Some also call it "moral injury" to capture the sense of having violated one's morals and the difficulty in making sense of their trauma in a way that allows one to go on with their life in a meaningful way.

Feeling guilty may also be a way of taking control again after experiencing a trauma, the very definition of which includes loss of power and control. When a trauma occurs, the world can feel unpredictable and blaming oneself for what happened can be a way of making other unwanted events predictable. Saying "it's my fault" may be a way of convincing yourself that you can stop it from happening again.

Sometimes people blame themselves for a trauma because it helps them maintain important relationships with others who have perpetrated the trauma. For example, a sexual assault survivor may need to maintain a relationship with their abuser. Telling yourself, "The abuse is my fault. If I did better, it wouldn't happen" is one way to maintain this relationship.

Unfortunately, while it makes sense that guilt and shame are such big parts of trauma, there is a cost to all of this. Guilt and shame can make symptoms and distress after trauma worse and keep people from recovering:

- The distress that comes up when you think about the guilt or what makes you feel guilty can compel you to avoid thinking about the trauma. This interferes with the "processing" of the trauma, which is critical to recovery. Processing means letting the natural reactions to the trauma run their course so that you can move forward.
- Left unchallenged, or unprocessed, conclusions you have drawn about your role in the trauma or its aftermath (e.g., "It's my fault, I should have ______, I must have deserved it ..."), start to seem like facts.
- When people feel guilty but don't examine it, the guilty feeling can spread to all areas of their lives and they may experience shame about who they are as a person (e.g., "I am a bad person"). This style of thinking can negatively affect how people live their life and prevent them from feeling close to others.
- People experience shame when thoughts such as, "I did something bad" become thoughts like, "I am bad." They may believe "I am unlovable" or even "I am a monster." They may think, "I don't deserve to feel better."

What is your reaction to all of this? What parts do you relate to?

[It is best to ask these questions after every bullet point or two to keep the client engaged and make this psychoeducation a conversation rather than a "lecture."]

3. More about guilt and shame and why we experience them

Why do we experience guilt?

One reason is that guilt can be adaptive in that it can help us learn from our experiences and figure out if there is anything we might do differently the next time we are in a similar situation.

When something bad happens, it's natural to momentarily feel guilty because that compels us to evaluate the situation to see if there is something we did that caused the event to happen. And if so, we learn not to do that again and we take steps to repair or make amends if we can and if it's appropriate.

Here is an example that's not related to trauma. Imagine that you are really rushed one morning and end up yelling at your loved one ***[or child, spouse, etc.—choose example relevant to your client]*** to hurry up and get out of the shower. You may feel guilty later. If you take the time to analyze why you feel this way, you may decide "That's not the kind of person I want to be. What can I do differently next time?" You may decide to apologize to your loved one and to wake up a little earlier or get some things ready the night before from now on.

If a parent misses their child's basketball game because they got held up or forgot, they may feel guilty. The guilt may compel them to leave earlier next time or create a reminder in their calendar.

So, guilt can be adaptive because it urges us to evaluate the situation and learn from it to increase our chances of a better outcome the next time something similar happens.

Another way guilt can be adaptive is that it serves as a beacon, shining a light on what is important to us, what our values are, and what we can decide to do to live according to our values in any given moment, regardless of whether or not we have for the past 5, 10, or 20 years.

Let's use an example of a parent who missed their child's basketball game. Examining why they feel guilty can allow them to identify what values they feel they have violated (such as being present for their child), and prompt them to make a commitment to do things differently in the future. For example, "I feel guilty because I didn't go to my child's game. I will change my schedule so I can make her big games in the future."

Have you ever changed your behavior or made plans to change your behavior because of something you felt guilty about? Can you give me an example?

Similarly, guilt may prevent us from acting in a way that violates our personal and/or societal values (e.g., that causes harm to another). It's an unpleasant feeling to say the least, so we want to avoid feeling it.

An example of this would be if I told my best friend I would take him out for his birthday but when the time came I wasn't in the mood. Being a good friend and keeping my commitments to my friends are important to me. These values may compel me to go even though I'm not in the mood.

Guilt can be a problem, though, when we don't have the opportunity to realistically evaluate and learn from what happened or take steps to make things better. What often happens instead is that we buy into the guilt, hook line, and sinker (e.g., "I feel guilty, therefore, I must have done something terribly wrong"). When we buy into it in this way, we give up the chance to find out if we really could have done something differently. In essence, instead of the guilt helping us guide our behavior in a value-driven way; the guilt starts to interfere with the way we live out life.

Does this seem true in terms of your experience with guilt? How so?

Why is it difficult to use guilt adaptively and let go of it sometimes?

When something as terrible as a traumatic event happens, it's very difficult to make sense of why it occurred. It's very common for people to blame themselves and tell themselves that if they had just made a better choice, they would have been able to prevent what happened. What we say to ourselves (our thoughts and beliefs), can be a contributing factor to guilt causing a great deal of pain and problems in our lives.

MILITARY/LAW ENFORCEMENT/FIRST RESPONDERS EXAMPLE

Your training may actually make it more likely that you feel guilt related to a trauma that occurred while in the line of duty or on deployment. Were you ever told that if something went wrong it was because you did something wrong? This is especially the case if you were in command or in charge (e.g., platoon leader), and you were taught that if anyone under you was hurt or did something wrong that it was your responsibility. This may also be the case if you were taught or told that it was your responsibility to protect or save anyone that was injured or in need (e.g., medic).

SEXUAL ASSAULT/ABUSE EXAMPLE

There are many messages in our society, media, and legal system that suggest that victims are at least partly to blame for being abused or assaulted—that they should have been able to avoid or stop the attack, or that they must have done something to bring it on. For example, what the victim was wearing, whether they were drinking or using drugs, where they were walking by themselves, whether they yelled or screamed or tried to get away, are all common questions people have when confronted with the disclosure of an assault. Being exposed to this all our lives, is it any wonder that we wind up blaming ourselves?

Because guilt and shame are very unpleasant feelings, it is common to avoid thinking about the guilt or the event that caused the guilt and shame.

Some trauma contexts encourage avoidance, meaning that the survivor does not want to think or talk about what happened and avoids people, places, or situations that remind them of what happened.

For example, in combat or in the line of duty, people have a job to do and may not be able to process the event until later.

Avoidance does not allow us to evaluate the situation and learn from it or to evaluate whether or not our conclusion that we are "guilty" is accurate.

So, guilt continues and can become shame.

We call this kind of guilt **Nonadaptive Guilt and Shame** or **NAGS** for short.

When you think about your trauma, and the guilt starts to come up, do you have a desire not to think about it?

What do you do so as not to think about it?

Therapist Tips

Sometimes clients don't immediately identify their avoidance or report doing the opposite of avoidance. That is, they spend a lot of time going over the trauma and feeling guilty. In this case, you would want to ask the client to describe their experience with rumination and present psychoeducation about it being a form of avoidance, such in the following suggested script.

"I am so glad you brought that up, because that is also quite common. We call that rumination. Just like you are describing it, rumination is when you focus on one or more aspects of the trauma that seems particularly important or upsetting. And on the surface, you're right, it can seem like you are giving the trauma a lot of attention, so you couldn't possibly be avoiding it. However, this type of 'thinking about it' actually leaves out some important pieces of the story that does not allow you to fully process or understand it."

How do we treat NAGS?

Now that we have talked about why guilt and shame cause pain and problems, let's talk about how we are going to address these in this therapy. First, we need to un-complicate guilt and shame.

- Guilt and shame are not pure emotions; they have a ***feeling*** part and a ***thinking*** part.
- The ***thinking*** part is influenced by our upbringing, past experiences (including other traumas), culture, our beliefs system, etc.
- The ***feeling*** part feels pretty bad—it makes it hard to think. Often there are other emotions involved besides just guilt or shame, like anger, sadness, grief, etc.

Do you experience any of these other feelings when you think about your trauma? Any other feelings?

In addition, when avoided, guilt and shame become one big messy glob of thoughts and feelings and it is hard to address until we break apart the feelings and thoughts.

We will work together to identify the thoughts that underlie your guilt and shame and break them down.

We are going to address each of these different types of thoughts in turn. We will look at different aspects of what happened during your trauma in order to do so. In this way, we will break up the glob and take a more complete look at what happened.

Does it make sense to you why we will be spending time looking at your traumatic experiences and guilt and shame feelings in this therapy? Can you explain your understanding of what we will be doing so I know that we are on the same page?

Tell me what questions and concerns you have about this process.

Homework Assignment

1. Reread sections of the workbook discussed this week.
2. Listen to the recording of this session at least once.
3. Make a list of any questions you may have about guilt and shame or about this therapy.

Close the Session

- What is one thing you got out of today?
- What are your reactions to today's session?

[The following are some suggested questions you may ask to address any concerns about the treatment commitment or motivation.]

What might get in the way of you completing your homework or you coming back next week?

Why is this important to you?

What would happen if you dropped out?

What would be the pros and cons of engaging or not engaging in this treatment? What would be the worst thing that could happen if you stuck with this and kept trying?

End Session

Session 2: Common Problems and Types of Guilt Related to Trauma

[Ask the client to start recording the session.]

Review Homework

- What stood out to you after the last session? What thoughts or questions did you have?
- How did listening to the session go? (What was it like to listen to the session? What struck you most as you listened to it? If not... what got in the way?)
- What were your thoughts about doing this therapy between the first session and today? Did you have any concerns or thoughts of not coming back? If so, how did you decide to come in today?
- What were some of the reasons that you came up with about why you want to engage in treatment?
- What do you want to get out of this intervention?

Session Agenda:

1. Present psychoeducation on trauma reactions and common problems.
2. Introduce the different types of guilt.
3. Start to discuss the client's experience with guilt.
4. Assign homework.
5. Close the session.

Last session we talked about guilt being very common after a traumatic event. We discussed how guilt can be adaptive in some cases and how it can be very distressing in others.

Any thoughts or questions about that before we continue?

Today, we are going to spend some time talking about some other common problems that people experience after trauma. We will also turn back to our discussion of guilt and talk about different types of guilt that can arise after traumatic events.

1. Share information on trauma reactions: Posttraumatic Stress Disorder (PTSD), Depression, Substance Use

A traumatic event is a situation where someone's life is at risk. Examples are situations where someone believes they or someone else will be killed, or when someone has a complete loss of power (like being held down and assaulted). Common examples include combat, physical and sexual assaults, car accidents, and natural disasters like fires and earthquakes.

What are some common problems people have after a traumatic event?

Most people feel very upset after they experience a trauma. They may keep remembering memories of the trauma even when they don't want to and have a hard time calming down or they may feel depressed. They may drink or use drugs more than usual to deal with their feelings after the trauma.

For many people, these problems get better after a couple of months, but for others they continue until the person gets treatment. Someone who feels a great deal of guilt or shame related to their trauma is more likely to continue having these problems.

When these problems do not go away, they may develop into PTSD, depression, or a substance use disorder. Let's spend some time talking about each of these problems and other kinds of problems people commonly have after trauma.

> **Therapist Tips**
> Spend more time on this information if this is the client's first treatment experience. We suggest asking clients what they know about each topic first and then filling in the information they missed or suggesting more accurate information if needed.

A. What is Post-traumatic Stress Disorder (PTSD)?

[Ask the client what they already know about PTSD. Use clinical judgment about whether or not there is a need to discuss symptoms in detail, particularly if the client clearly does not have this diagnosis. When appropriate, introduce the four PTSD symptom clusters and associated features, asking the client if and how they experience each. Refer client to appropriate page in their Workbook as you go over these. Note that it is not unusual for people to experience some, but not all, of these symptoms. Also note that some symptoms may have been more severe at first but improved overtime (e.g., startle response), while others may have persisted or gotten worse (e.g., irritability and guilt).]

PTSD is when someone is still deeply bothered by a trauma months or years after it happened. They may try not to think about it or avoid reminders of it, yet have parts of it pop up in their memory when they do not want it throughout the day or in nightmares. They may be more on edge or alert because of the trauma and may even have trouble sleeping or concentrating. Importantly, the way someone views themselves or the world can change because of the trauma, such as feeling guilt and shame. Having thoughts like "I'm not as good a person as I thought I was" and "I don't deserve to be happy" are perfect examples of this.

Your workbook lists the symptoms of PTSD. If you'd like to talk about them in more detail, please let me know.

Tell me about your experiences with PTSD symptoms. What gets in the way of living your life/bothers you most?

B. What is Depression?

[Introduce the symptoms, asking client if and how they experience each.]

Feeling down or depressed is very common following a traumatic event. This may be related to grief or loss if the trauma involved the death of someone close to you. Some people also report feeling like they have lost a part of themselves. It may also be related to having difficulty resuming your usual activities and feeling as if life has lost some of its meaning.

Depression can be a part of PTSD but it can also be a separate problem, especially when the depressed mood is accompanied by difficulty sleeping, loss of interest in activities you used to enjoy, changes in appetite/weight, low energy/motivation, feelings of worthlessness, and frequent thoughts of death or that you would be better off dead. For some people, these symptoms can last for weeks or even months, making it really hard to function.

Does any of this sound familiar to you? Which parts?

C. What is a Substance Use Disorder?

[Introduce the symptoms, asking client if and how they experience each.]

Drinking alcohol or using other substances is also common following trauma. Sometimes people wind up drinking or using drugs in order to get to sleep, to be able to be around people easier, or to quell the distressing feelings, memories, and/or thoughts in their minds. This is often called "self-medication."

Sometimes people feel like they don't care about anything anymore or don't deserve better and drinking or using drugs is a way of escaping or even harming themselves.

Can you relate to these ideas?

What substances, if any, have you used in these ways?

What may be helpful in the short run can turn into a problem of its own in the long run. Substance use can lead to many negative consequences (e.g., legal problems, relationship problems, and health problems) and, most importantly, interferes with recovery from the pain of traumatic experiences, including guilt and shame.

How do these symptoms and diagnoses (e.g., PTSD, depression, and substance use disorder) affect your guilt and shame?

[If indicated, ask "Have you experienced any not so good consequences related to your use of ______?"]

[If indicated, "There is more information in your Workbook about substance use problems if you are interested in learning more."]

[If needed, you can use the following prompts: "Have you ever felt shame because of your drinking/substance use?" "Do you ever feel like there is something wrong with you when you feel you can't handle something you used to be able to?"]

Cycle of Post-traumatic Distress: Trauma Reactions and What Maintains Them?

Before we go into your experience in more detail, let's talk more broadly about what happens to someone during a traumatic (life threatening) event.

What happens when human beings (or any animal) perceive a threat?

When we perceive a threat our mind and body go into survival mode. The fight-flight-freeze response gets activated. Do you know what that is?

When we perceive danger, our sympathetic nervous system switches on—it's automatic.

Our mind and body quickly prepares itself to do whatever it takes to survive the threat, which means freezing, fighting, or fleeing. So, in case we will need to fight or flee, we become quickly prepared in the following ways:

- Our heart rate and breathing get faster, to get more oxygen and blood to big muscle groups.
- Blood flows to big muscle groups and parts of the brain that are charged with this survival mechanism, and away from extremities and higher functioning brain areas, which explains why you might feel tingling and/or like you don't have full control of your thinking, or things are surreal.
- Eyesight and hearing become more sensitive, so that we can better detect additional signs of danger and/or survival aids.
- Nonessential systems, like our digestive system, pause to preserve energy, and our body gets rid of excess weight (by evacuating bowels/bladder).

Do you recall going into the fight-flight-freeze response during your trauma?

Which of the physiological responses we just discussed did you feel during trauma?

What else did you experience?

[You will likely come back to this information in Module 2 since guilt may stem from the beliefs that the person failed because of these physiological reactions, e.g., "I failed because I froze."]

Finally, after the perceived threat has passed and we have survived, our body goes back into "rest mode" and the fight-flight-freeze response turns off. When this happens, we start feeling relatively more relaxed, maybe even tired and sleepy, hungry, thirsty, and shaky.

Who is at risk of developing mental health problems or suffering after trauma?

Most people feel a lot of distress and suffer some of the symptoms we have discussed after a trauma, but many people recover from this after a few months. Certain factors can get in the way/make it more likely that you develop PTSD or one or more of the other problems we have discussed:

One of the major factors that contributes to ongoing post-traumatic distress is avoidance:

- Avoiding thinking about what happened, having feelings about it, or avoiding situations that remind you of what happened can be helpful in the short term. You might feel immediate relief when you have gotten out of something you were dreading. But avoidance is not helpful in the long run—it maintains post-traumatic distress and can even make it worse overtime.

[Use example that is most relevant to the client]

COMBAT OR MOTOR VEHICLE ACCIDENT EXAMPLE

A common example of this is when someone's trauma involved a car accident or an explosion that included the smell of gas or diesel fuel. They may start to avoid going to gas stations because the smell of gas makes them upset or feel on edge. Going to a gas station in and of itself is not dangerous, but it feels dangerous to this person because the smell of gas is a reminder of the trauma.

SEXUAL ASSAULT EXAMPLE

If someone was sexually assaulted in bed, they may start to associate the bed and nighttime with danger and find it very difficult to feel safe enough to sleep in a bed. But a bed and nighttime are in and of themselves not dangerous, nor are they a sign that danger is imminent. They are reminders of the trauma and avoiding them does not allow for processing of the event and the associations that go along with it.

The other major contributor to ongoing post-traumatic distress is what you tell yourself about the trauma; what your interpretations are about why it happened, what or who caused it, your role in it, your reactions during or after, etc.

[Reminder to use client's examples as much as possible]:

After a traumatic event, it is pretty common for people to have thoughts like:

- About the trauma: *This should never have happened.*
- Why it happened: *It happened because I did something wrong, or I didn't listen to my instinct (I knew something bad was going to happen). I was not properly prepared. I deserved it/had it coming.*
- Your reaction: *I failed, I should have done more. I was paralyzed and that means I'm a failure. I felt nothing and that means I'm a monster. I didn't tell anyone, so that must mean I wanted it to happen.*
- Your role in it: *It was my fault. I should have been able to stop it. I should have known this was going to happen.*
- What it means about you, others, the world, the future: *I am evil, I am damaged goods or defective, people are evil and cannot be trusted, I let people down, the world is dangerous and no one can be counted on.*

Do any of these thoughts sound familiar? Are there similar things that you say to yourself?

[Assisting the client with walking through their interpretations of the trauma, their perceived role, and how their thoughts have changed following the event is an ample place to start to identify guilt-related cognitions. Reminder to write down any guilt thoughts the client identifies in the Guilt and Shame Cognitions Log in their workbook.]

What you have been telling yourself about the trauma and how you see yourself now are what we will be focusing on in this therapy.

2. Different Types of Trauma-Related Guilt/NAGS

There are many different ways that someone might experience guilt related to trauma. Some of these might apply to you and others not so much. Let me know which ones seem to speak to your experience of guilt.

[Choose types of guilt to discuss and related examples relevant to the client's experiences. Refer client to this section in their workbook. After each example, discuss to what extent they apply to the client.]

a. **Negligence/betrayal/abandonment guilt**: Behaving negligently (e.g., neglecting or not doing one's job, falling asleep when on patrol or at the wheel, leaving a friend at a party who then gets sexually assaulted, and having a loved one commit suicide) or not doing enough or more in a situation. Two underlying assumptions of this kind of guilt are that: (1) you were capable of doing more and thus should have done more, and (2) what you actually did was not effective.

Do you feel this kind of guilt?

If yes, What do you believe you were negligent about?

b. Incompetence/superman/superwoman guilt: Believing that you can control uncontrollable physiological responses, like your body's automatic response to a perceived threat (e.g., freezing instead of fighting). Underneath this kind of guilt is a belief that you should have been able to make everything right, you should have been able to save the day. This type of guilt can occur when one's actions were impacted by fear, honest mistakes, accidents, inexperience, or inadequate training, and not actual guilt or wrongdoing. The natural and adaptive fight-flight-freeze response phenomenon often can explain behaviors that fall in this category.

Another example is when people come to believe that they had known at the time how things would turn out. Or that they could have controlled how things turned out and therefore should have made a different decision, when in fact they actually did not know or have control at the time. People will sometimes say they saw warning signs and should have listened to them, but they are not taking into account all of the other information they had to consider at the time.

Tell me what kinds of beliefs you have about you should have been able to do during your traumatic experience.

[If endorsed, may want to review fight-flight-freeze response.]

Do you believe you knew or should have known the outcome and/or that you had the capacity to change the outcome?

[If yes, Tell me about that? What exactly do you remember knowing for certain?]

c. Survivor or leaving guilt: Feeling guilt for living when someone else died or leaving a dangerous situation when others had to stay behind. Medical personnel can experience this kind of guilt when someone dies in their care.

Have you experienced this kind of guilt? Do you now?

d. Feeling pleasure or nothing during a trauma: When a person experiences a rush or overwhelming sense of pleasure after killing or harming another, or feels nothing (no remorse), and believes this is not normal or means there is something wrong with them. In fact, this reaction is normal and is a response to having a threat removed which is understandably relieving. In addition, any excess energy left over from the Fight-Flight-Freeze survival response can contribute to feeling a rush of pleasure or joy once the threat has been eliminated. Our brains might interpret this feeling of joy as being attributed to the negative parts of the trauma (e.g., killing someone).

Another example of this kind of guilt is common in sexual abuse survivors. It is not uncommon for people to have enjoyed some parts of it. For example, many people report that it felt good to get attention, to feel loved, special (this is really common in cases where they might not have much attention or love anywhere else). In addition, when certain parts of our body, namely those involved in sex, are stimulated we feel arousal and pleasure, whether we like it or not. This can produce a lot of confusion and shame. Some people describe feeling betrayed by their body.

Do you recall feeling good after doing something you ordinarily would not be happy about doing?

e. Atrocity guilt: Observing or participating in a terrible, horrific act against another human being. Because such an act is so wrong and unjustifiable, it leads someone to come to the conclusion that their entire character must be flawed. Usually, the person feeling guilty does not take into account that even humane (i.e., kind and compassionate) people with high moral standards can behave inhumanely under certain conditions. Or that some situations elicit certain behaviors that would otherwise be unacceptable and unthinkable to a person.

Have you ever heard of the Stanford Prison Experiment? A group of normal, average male college students were assigned to act as prisoners or prison guards, totally at random, in a fake prison environment. Prisoners started acting like real prisoners (eyes down, learned helplessness) and guards started acting like stereotypical guards (degrading, bossing around, even torturing to some extent—with a water hose). It got so bad the researchers stopped the experiment. Remember that these were normal college kids and each one could have just as easily been assigned to be a guard as a prisoner—the two groups did not differ before the experiment. This suggests that people react very similarly given the right (or wrong) conditions.

f. **Self-blame to maintain an important relationship**: It is common to place blame on oneself in order to be able to maintain a relationship with someone who has some power and control. For example, abused children often believe they are being abused because they did something wrong. It is easier for them to maintain attachment to their parent on whom they depend for food, a home, etc., if they blame themselves for the abuse instead of the parent. It is easier to maintain a relationship with someone if you blame yourself instead of them.

   Do you think this might apply to you?

   [If yes, In what way might you have been dependent on .... e.g., the perpetrator, group, institution in which the trauma occurred]?

g. **Not reporting the assault (or other crime against you or someone else)**: This is a common source of guilt in physical or sexual assault survivors who believe they could have prevented future assaults to themselves or others. What the survivor typically is not recalling is all of the reasons why they did not, or could not, take action.

   What are other reasons people might feel guilty about a trauma they experienced? Is there anything you feel guilty about that is not covered by the types of guilt we just discussed?

3. Your Experience with Guilt

A deep sense of responsibility may be helpful to get you through a traumatic situation, but may be hurting you now, after the trauma has long been over. Examining the events now can help you make meaning from what happened in a way you couldn't when the event occurred.

Are there aspects of guilt that may have been or are helpful to you?

How is guilt hurting your life or others or things/people that are important to you?

Therapist Tips
The client may not understand how aspects of the way they are experiencing guilt could be helpful to them, or the function behind their guilt. The clinician can start to assist the client in this understanding (e.g., belief that feeling guilty helps the client remember the person they lost, helps remind them they are not a monster, and keeps them from doing something "bad" again). You will continue to explore this with the client over the course of the intervention, and Module 3 has a section that explicitly addresses it.

Introduce Guilt and Shame Cognitions Log

[Refer client to the Guilt and Shame Cognitions Log in the Workbook]

This log will be a place for you to write down thoughts you are having when you feel guilt or shame. Jot down anything that seems related to guilt as close as possible to when you're experiencing or thinking about it, just like we've already started to do in here. This will be your homework assignment for the week, to track any guilt or shame thoughts and feelings you have regarding your trauma. For now, that's all I want you to do.

Don't try to do anything with these thoughts and feelings. Allow yourself to have them; don't try to change them or push them away. But you can start considering the possibility that your thoughts/beliefs/conclusions may not be 100% accurate. That other thoughts, beliefs, or conclusions are possible, and that may be more accurate.

Do give this homework some serious thought—the more guilt thoughts you are able to identify the more we will have to work with in this therapy. Here are some common guilt and shame-related beliefs people have about traumatic experiences:

- I should have known better.
- I should/shouldn't have done/said....
- Why did/didn't I...?
- I had no reason to...
- I did something wrong when I...
- It's my fault that ... happened, because I ...
- I don't deserve anything good.
- I deserved ***[the trauma, or other bad things]*** to happen.

Homework Assignment

1. Reread sections of the workbook discussed this week.
2. Listen to the recording of the session at least once.
3. Identify and list guilt cognitions on log. Try to do this each day.

Close the Session

- What is one thing you got out of today?
- What are your reactions to today's session?

[The following are some suggested questions you may ask to address any concerns about the treatment commitment or motivation.]

What might get in the way of you completing your homework or you coming back next week?

Why is this important to you?

What would happen if you dropped out?

What would be the pros and cons of engaging or not engaging in this treatment? What would be the worst thing that could happen if you stuck with this and kept trying?

End Session

MODULE 2, SESSIONS 3 AND 4

Debriefing the traumatic event and appraising trauma-related guilt and shame

Sessions 3 and 4: Guilt appraisal

The main focus of this module is to help the clients examine their beliefs about the trauma that bring about guilt and shame. The goal is to help the clients develop a broader perspective of the trauma and their role, something they have not been able to do fully because of avoidance and inaccurate beliefs. This process helps to resolve maladaptive guilt and shame and helps the clients to move forward with less suffering in regard to their role in the trauma.

Throughout the chapter, we give examples relevant to survivors of different kinds of traumas. You do not have to present all of the examples. Feel free to use the most relevant ones for your client or modify these or use your own. These examples can be adapted to be relevant to many other types of trauma.

Module 2 usually takes two sessions to complete. The second session can be used to continue working on the first trauma or to process a second trauma. Some clients have several traumas about which they feel guilty and the therapist may decide a third session is needed to complete Module 2.

[Remind client to begin recording session]

Review Homework

- What stood out to you after the last session, the readings? What thoughts or questions did you have?
- How did listening to the session go? What was it like to listen to the session? What struck you most as you listened to it? (If not… what got in the way of listening to the session?)
- What were your thoughts about doing this therapy between last session and today?
- Review list of guilt cognitions (Guilt and Shame Cognitions Log). ***[Have client open workbook to their log.]***

Trauma Informed Guilt Reduction Therapy
https://doi.org/10.1016/B978-0-12-814780-1.09984-6

Session Agenda:
1. Examine guilt in a systematic way
2. Start to explore the relationship between guilt and the client's important values
3. Assign Homework
4. Close Session

Introduce guilt appraisal: A systematic way of examining guilt and shame

Do you remember how we discussed that guilt is complicated? Guilt involves bad or unpleasant feelings, but it also involves a set of beliefs, thoughts, interpretations, and negative value judgments about the self. And it's even more complicated than that. In fact, there are many different ways to define guilt, and therefore, to conclude that you are guilty.

Guilt is like a big messy blob. It's confusing, heavy, and emotionally intense. It's hard to make sense out of it.

Have you noticed whether you are better at making sense out of things when you are experiencing very strong emotions or when your emotions are more moderate? For example, do you have your best ideas when you are very angry? It turns out that when we feel any emotion very strongly, it's more difficult to be very rational or reasonable.

So, the first step we want to take is to separate out the distress or emotional pain associated with guilt. Let's take a few moments to identify the emotions that you experience when you think about this traumatic event.

Therapist Tips

The therapist helps the client identify emotions that they may experience when they think of the trauma (e.g., anger, shame, guilt, sadness, confusion).

During the guilt appraisal, we ask the client to set their emotional experiences aside. By taking the time to identify the client's emotions, the therapist can help redirect the clients to the task at hand when they become emotionally activated.

During the guilt appraisal, we are going to ask you to try to look at your trauma memory without having emotions drive the experience. Essentially, we are going to have you put your emotions off to the side. It's not that feelings are not important, or that you shouldn't feel them. In fact, quite the opposite, but as you know, strong feelings get in the way of thinking clearly so we just want to put a little distance between them, turn the volume down a little, only for the time being.

You might have also noticed that guilt that is related to a trauma is different than the type of guilt that happens in normal everyday life because trauma-related guilt causes profound distress.

Do you remember why I am asking you to do this?

[If the client is unable to recall some of the reasons trauma-related guilt can become maladaptive with intense emotions, briefly review the Nonadaptive Guilt and Shame (NAGS) model, referring the client to Module 1 in their workbook]

There are many different ways to define guilt, and therefore, to conclude that you are guilty. The most common ways are:

1. Foreseeability and Preventability (Hindsight Bias): Believing the trauma was foreseeable and therefore preventable.
2. Insufficient Justification: Thinking you were not justified in doing what you did. That there were not good reasons to do what you did and that there were other better options.
3. Causal Responsibility: Feeling mostly or fully responsible for what happened yourself, your action or inaction during the trauma.
4. Violation of Values (Wrongdoing): Believing that you purposely caused what happened.

It may still be difficult to understand guilt when we break it apart, but it is easier to understand than when all the parts are fused together. As we examine your guilt one piece at a time, it will become clearer.

With increased clarity comes increased freedom, allowing you to be more flexible in how you respond to the trauma memory. For example, you can focus on your values and committing to live in line with them, which is what we will discuss in the latter part of therapy.

In this therapy, we are going to examine and analyze your guilt by evaluating each part of your guilt, one at a time, in a logical way. Our goal is to help you reach an accurate, objective, and realistic appraisal of your role in the trauma.

We're not trying to fool you into believing something that is not true just to make you feel better. While it might be nice to feel better, that wouldn't last.

Instead, we're going to look at the actual evidence for what you're telling yourself that is causing guilt.

Just as we need to break guilt apart to get a better handle on it, we need to look at one source of guilt at a time. I'm going to ask you now to tell me about the most distressing source of guilt related to your trauma.

> **Therapist Tips**
> The clients may express they are supposed to feel guilty and/or ashamed about what happened, thus they do not want to let go of the guilt/shame. The therapist should remind the client that the goal is not to take away the client's guilt; but to see if there are more adaptive ways to understand their experience. If helpful, review the differences between NAGS and adaptive guilt and shame from Module 1 to help reinforce that it is not the goal of the clinician to take away the client's guilt.

Recounting the trauma: Understanding the source of the guilt

[Ask the clients to describe in detail the events of their trauma-specific events that led up to their decisions, and factors they took into consideration at the time they were making decisions.]

> **Therapist Tips**
> Although we do not suggest a specific amount of time to spend going through the trauma account, we encourage you to keep the account brief. The purpose of the trauma account is for the client to provide enough information for you to understand the source of their guilt and shame. You will continue to use Socratic questions to understand the trauma in greater detail during each portion of the guilt appraisal.

Give me a slow-motion description of what happened leading up to the trauma and what happened during the trauma itself. Tell me exactly what happened, leading up to the specific day, situation, incident, or point in time when you thought that you should/shouldn't have ______.

During the retelling, just focus on the historical facts and try to make no value judgments about what happened. I only want you to tell me the facts of what happened. What did you see, hear, feel, smell during the trauma? What did you know and what did you not know at that time? Who did what, who said what, what thoughts went through your mind—leading up to that specific point in time—that day?

[After the client is finished recounting the trauma...]

What is the main thing you think you should have done differently or shouldn't have done?

When you think back on it now, at what point in this event does the first "should" thought pop into your mind? When is the first time you think you should/shouldn't have ________?

Tell me how you think you should have acted differently?

When did you first realize or learn that this was what you were supposed to do?

[You can use the following prompts to help the clients recall the situation and their thoughts and feelings at the time. Ask as few or as many of these as you find helpful.]

- What was the worst part of the story you just told me?
- What were your feelings during the worst part?
- What were your thoughts during the worst part?
- What should you have known better?
- What are some of the negative outcomes you could have prevented?
- What should you have done differently? Describe exactly what you think you should have done and when you should have done this?

Therapist Tips

The first "should" or "shouldn't" thought that a client shares may not be the one that is bothering them the most. You may need to use a "downward arrow" technique to help get to the thought that is causing the most distress for the client. As the clients share "should" or "shouldn't" thoughts, you can ask "What bothers you most about that?" or "Why should/shouldn't you have done that?" Until you have identified the most distressing thought.

For example, in our work with Veterans, a common first thought is "I shouldn't have killed the insurgent." On further questioning, we discover the thought that truly haunts the client is "I shouldn't have enjoyed it" or "I should have known he was a civilian." Sometimes, it isn't until you are further along in the debrief that you discover that you are not working on the most troubling thought. It is fine to acknowledge this to the client and say, "It seems like maybe what is bothering you the most isn't that you shouldn't have killed him, but that you shouldn't have enjoyed it? Is that right?" If the client agrees, we recommend starting the debrief over and working on the should/shouldn't thought that truly is the most painful to the person.

Therapist Tips

The following are examples of how your client might respond.

Sexual Assault: *I shouldn't have led him on, I always said hello and asked him how his day was. If I wasn't so friendly I would never have been assaulted. I first started thinking this while I was at the hospital, and my coworkers came to visit me.*

Military Combat Trauma: *I shouldn't have let the convoy go left, if we had gone right instead the IED would not have gone off and my friend would be alive. I started thinking this when I was back in the states, there was no time to think while I was in Iraq.*

Suicide: *I should have never had a gun in the house. I knew the risks, guns kill people. It's my fault my spouse is dead. This was the first thought I had when I found her.*

This is not the time for the therapist to start to challenge these thoughts. The client will learn to evaluate their own thoughts in a systematic way in each of the guilt and shame appraisal sections. Remember—we want the client to start to change their beliefs on their own with the guidance of the therapist.

[Once you have identified the "should" or "shouldn't" have thought you are going to work on, have the client complete the AAGS for that thought.]

Remember we discussed the types of guilt common after trauma?

[Refer the client to The Different Types of Trauma-Related Guilt/NAG section in their workbook]

a. Negligence/betrayal/abandonment

b. Incompetence/superman/superwoman

c. Surviving or leaving

d. Feeling pleasure or nothing from killing or hurting someone

e. Committing or witnessing atrocities

f. Blaming yourself to maintain an important relationship

g. Not reporting illegal or deviant behavior

Which categories does your guilt fall into? Does it fall into more than one?

Let's look more closely at your guilt to evaluate it one part at a time.

> **Therapist Tips**
> It is typically most effective, just like conducting any cognitive therapy, to start with the most distressing guilt cognition(s).
>
> The therapist can introduce and use role plays or role reversals during each of the appraisal skills to assist the client in evaluating and challenging their guilt. For example, asking the client to think about what they might say to their best friend who reported having the same guilt thought can make it easier for them to think logically about it.

1. Foreseeability/Preventability Analysis

[Refer the client to this section in their Workbook]

One of the ways that we conclude that we're guilty is we believe that what happened was foreseeable, that we could and should have seen it coming. And, if we believe it was foreseeable then that means it was also preventable, meaning that we could have stopped it from happening. So, if we believe it was preventable and we didn't prevent it, it means we allowed it to happen.

[Check for understanding]

Does that make sense to you?

Well, let's see if that's true in this case. We'll perform what we call a "foreseeability and preventability analysis."

You may not have known as much as you think you knew. In other words, perhaps the negative outcome that you think was foreseeable and therefore preventable may not have been as foreseeable as you think it was. This is called "hindsight bias." Have you ever heard of that?

Hindsight bias occurs when knowledge of an event's outcome (e.g., who won a sporting event) distorts or biases a person's memory of what they knew before the outcome was known. Hindsight biased thinking is similar to "Monday morning quarterbacking":

- Friends discussing last night's game are more likely to report having known the winning team was going to win, even if this is not the case. Really, if they had known, wouldn't they have bet all their life savings on the game?

It turns out that this is a human phenomenon. We all do this. Multiple research studies with average people found that people are likely to say that they knew who was going to win after the game. This happens even if you tell them about hindsight bias and they assure you that they are reporting accurately on who they thought was going to win before the game was even played.

It's hard not to let information we know now, after the game, cloud our memory of what we actually did or did not know in the past. We bring the information we have today along with us when we think of the past. And when we're judging something we did or didn't do in the past, we base that judgment on what we know now. So, after knowing the outcome of an event, we tend to remember having more knowledge than we actually had prior to the event's conclusion.

But is that a fair conclusion when we did not have the outcome information at the time of the trauma/decision?

As applied to trauma, many survivors falsely believe that the events were foreseeable and therefore preventable, so they blame themselves for not having prevented the situation from occurring. Sound familiar?

Hindsight bias is evident by statements such as, "I should have known better," "I should have done something differently," "I saw it coming," "I knew what was going to happen (before outcomes were known)," and "I could have prevented it."

SEXUAL ASSAULT/ABUSE EXAMPLE

A woman's colleague asks to meet with her privately to work on a project. She finds her colleague to be friendly and is happy about the meeting thinking that this is her opportunity to move ahead in the business. The colleague sexually assaults her and she then blames herself for agreeing to meet with her coworker. "I should have known he was going to assault me. I should have refused to meet with him. I deserved what happened because I met with him for selfish reasons (getting ahead)." She neglects to remember that she didn't know, and did not have reason to know, that her colleague was going to assault her.

COMBAT MILITARY EXAMPLE

A driver on a convoy was assigned to do surveillance on a particular area. At one point, he decided to turn the convoy left instead of right, as he worried there might be an IED on the road to the right. An IED exploded on the road to the left, killing people in one of the trucks in the convoy. He blames himself saying "I should have known there was an IED on that road. I should have gone the other way." He neglects to remember that he worried there might be an IED in the other direction too.

SUICIDE EXAMPLE

A man comes home to find his wife has committed suicide with the family gun. The gun is kept in a lock box in the home, unloaded, for protection from intruders. Both the man and his wife have been trained how to use the weapon and purchased the weapon after there was a series of break-ins in their neighborhood several years before. The man blames himself for having the gun in the home and believes that he could have prevented his wife's death. He neglects to remember that his spouse has never talked about suicide, had not attempted suicide previously, and that the gun has been in their home for years without incident.

Hindsight-biased thinking is also signaled by phrases such as, "There were warning signs," "There were red flags (signaling what was going to happen)," "There were clues," "At some level, I knew what was going to happen," and "I felt like something was wrong." But have you ever been faced with a red flag, or thought something was going to happen and it didn't? Red flags are just that, red flags, they are not certainty. There might have been red flags but there certainly were other pieces of information that were signaling different things.

Of course, there are sometimes red flags, or signs, or a hunch that something bad might happen. But these are rarely the only pieces of information available at the time. We typically have many pieces of information to consider and based on which to decide. In reality, acting on hunches rarely pays off. We have all sorts of thoughts all the time. For example, "My team hasn't won in a long time, maybe today is their day" doesn't mean it will pay off to bet your life savings on your team today. If your team does finally win today, that is not evidence that you should in fact have bet your life savings, because most likely you would have lost it!

To sum up, you can only prevent something if you knew it was going to happen, AND if you have the option and the ability to prevent it. You are only capable of preventing something if that something is foreseeable.

So, in the case of your trauma, did you really know what was going to happen?

[Ask the client to talk through what they did know at the time of the trauma. "Why did you do what you did at the time of the trauma? Without knowing what you know today, only knowing what you knew at the time?" Ask questions to further probe what they actually did or did not know.

- ***Sexual Assault—"What were the reasons you believed his intent was to work on the project?"***

- ***Combat Military—"Did you have the power to change the convoy's route? What did you think might happen if you went the other way?"***
- ***Suicide—"When you left that morning, was this day different from other days?"]***

A good way to check whether something was foreseeable is to ask yourself this Million Dollar Question: If you knew with certainty what was going to happen when you did what you did, would you have done what you did? If the answer is no, that's proof you did not know what was going to happen.

There is no possible way that you could have foreseen ***[the negative outcome]***. Otherwise, you wouldn't have done what you did.

Re-answer item #1 from the AAGS

So, let's review how you answered the question related to this on the AAGS. What is the answer that reality would dictate, that a judge and jury would conclude is the correct answer based on the evidence of what you knew and didn't know before the trauma happened?

The first time you circled your answer. Now answer the item again, this time with a triangle around your answer.

[Most of the time, the clients select a lower level of hindsight bias on this item than they previously endorsed. If your client does not, probe for additional hindsight bias and continue to address if needed.]

What are you feeling now?

[The clients may or may not talk about guilt at this time but may acknowledge they couldn't have known what to do at the time to prevent the trauma from occurring. If the client does bring up guilt, the client may logically understand the difference but may not FEEL less guilty. Normalize this and reinforce that feelings may start to shift as they continue through the guilt appraisal. It is important that the therapist does not force this process. Remember, the goal is not to reduce guilt but to help your client develop an accurate appraisal of what happened.]

2. Justification Analysis

Another set of thinking errors that can contribute to the NAGS is related to how justified we think we are in doing what we did, in making the choices we made.

[Refer the client to Lack of Justification section in the Workbook]

The most justified choice in any situation is the best course of action among the courses of action you had available to you and considered at the time. It's similar to answering a multiple-choice test. The instructions say to circle the best answer. The most justified answer—the answer for which you have the best reasons—is one of the four choices provided—a, b, c, or d.

What happens if you write in, "choice e?" Would you get credit? No, you won't. You can only choose one of the available choices. This is what we do when we judge a choice we have made in the past against an idealized or better choice that was not available at that time. In other words, idealized options or courses of action that were not available or actually considered (at the time) cannot be used to evaluate justifiability (goodness of reasons for acting as you did in the situation).

Similarly, weighing the actions you took against options that came to mind later is also not fair.

For example, let's say I'm deciding on a move. My choices are North Carolina or South Carolina. You help me weigh the pros and cons of both places and we both come to an agreement that North Carolina is the best of the two options. So, I move there and a week later I call you up and chew you out: "You were so wrong! I should have moved to Georgia!"

What's your reaction to that? Right, "What the…?? Georgia??!! That wasn't one of the options!" So, a "should" statement there on my part is inaccurate.

SEXUAL ASSAULT/ABUSE EXAMPLE

Your husband is assaulting you nightly. Never having married him is not an option because it is not an available choice at the time of the trauma.

COMBAT MILITARY EXAMPLE

You're facing a situation of kill or be killed in combat. "I shouldn't have enlisted" is not an option at the time of the trauma.

SUICIDE EXAMPLE

Your family member killed himself while home alone. Staying with them 24 hours a day/7 days per week was not an option.

Another type of thinking error that leads us to conclude we were not justified is ignoring what we thought about each of the options available to us at the time. Although we know the outcome now, at the time each option that was available had the pros and cons that may have looked very different in the moment than they do now.

SEXUAL ASSAULT/ABUSE EXAMPLE

The client freezes during a sexual assault. They tell you they believe they could have stopped the assault had they fought back. They may not be considering that had they fought back, they may have been more severely injured or experienced more pain during the assault.

COMBAT MILITARY EXAMPLE

The client is faced with the situation of having to kill an armed child during war, their belief is "no child should be harmed." They may not be considering that had they not shot, they would have put themselves and many others for whom they were responsible at great risk of harm.

SUICIDE EXAMPLE

The client is the first person to find a family member following a suicide; their belief is "I shouldn't have gone to work that day." They may not be considering that they would have lost their job had they not gone in that day, or there were many other mornings their family member was similarly depressed but did not commit suicide.

So, I'm going to ask you to remember the options you had at the time and then we'll examine what the pros and cons of each were.

Therapist Tips

Use the Justification Analysis Worksheet in the workbook. Across the top row, assist the clients in listing the options they considered and were available to them at the time. Option A should be the course of action they took. You may have to prime the clients repeatedly to focus only on what they knew at the time, as they have had a lot of time since the trauma to think about what they should or shouldn't have done.

What were your reasons for doing what you did? What other courses of action did you consider at the time?

Next, ask the client to record the pros and cons for each option they listed in the top row. For each "alternative" course of action that was considered at the time of the trauma, ask the client the following:

Knowing only what you knew then (before outcomes were known) what did you think (at the time) would have happened had you done that?

Why did you rule that choice (course of action) out?

> What were the pros and cons of each of these options?
>
> Optional: It is very common for clients to have a hard time coming up with options other than what they did. If what the client did was the only course of action the client considered, conduct an additional justification analysis comparing what he or she did with the alternative course of action that occurred to them only later. Only include options in the analysis that were truly possible at the time. This can help challenge the belief that the other options would have resulted in only a positive outcome.

So, was there a best choice (or if there was no good choice, the "least bad choice") among the courses of action that you considered at the time? ***[If appropriate…]*** What were your reasons for making the choice you made? Do you think the decision you made was justified based on the information that you had at the time?

It is also important to consider whether things really would have turned out better had you done something else that was possible at the time. In other words, you think that if you had just done ______________ ***[use your client's own words]*** everything would have turned out so much better, right? But how do you know that? What were the cons of the other options? Is it possible that something even worse than what happened might have happened?

[It is especially important to cover the next two points if the client continues to question what the best option was.]

In heightened/increased states of arousal, our ability to think clearly and make logical decisions are very impaired. When people experience trauma, they are on automatic survival mode and they have only three choices: fight, flight, or freeze. And, your survival system decides which is your best bet, based on prior experiences (what might have helped you survive in prior threat experiences), and current context. It's not really in your hands.

Also, the capacity for complex thinking and problem solving goes out the window. So, while you might be an excellent problem solver with the ability to come up with 21 different options and weigh all their pros and cons accurately when you are relatively relaxed, this is impossible when you are under threat or in shock. So, it's important to consider your emotional state when you were making this decision before you can judge it. Do you recall how you were feeling at the time? How might that have been impairing your judgment?

Finally, experiencing a trauma and trauma-related guilt makes it easier to see only the negative aspects of what happened. Those things are what we remember. But there may be the pros to your choices too. What were some of the pros of the action you took?

[Revisit options and their pros and cons on Justification Worksheet in workbook as needed.]

So, again, what was the best choice (or if there was no good choice, the "least bad choice") among the courses of action that you considered at the time? ***[If appropriate…]*** The decision you made was the most justified choice based upon the information you had at the time and how your body was responding to that information.

It can be difficult to accept this when the outcome was so negative. When none of the options available were good ones. But that doesn't mean that what you did was not the best course of action given the options you had at the time.

Re-answer item #2 from the AAGS

So let's review how you answered the question related to this on the AAGS. What is the answer that reality would dictate, that a judge and jury would conclude is the correct answer based on the evidence of what was the best option out of those you had at the time?

The first time you circled your answer. Now answer the item again, this time with a triangle around your answer.

[Most of the time, the clients choose an item indicating better justification for their actions than they did previously. If not, continue to probe for thoughts that may not have been addressed yet.]

What are your reactions to the justification analysis?

[Again, you do not need to bring up guilt unless the client does. The client may logically understand the difference but may not FEEL less guilty. Normalize this. It is essential that the therapist does not force this process.]

3. Responsibility Analysis

[Do not try to convince the client that they are not responsible for their actions. Rather, try to help the client make the distinction between responsibility and blame, and zoom out and consider all the factors that contributed to the outcome.]

Next, we'll conduct a responsibility analysis. Responsibility is often another way we assign guilt to ourselves. First, we are going to look at the difference between responsibility and blame. We often get these confused.

- For example, blaming a child for spilling milk implies the child did something wrong. The child might have done something to cause the milk to spill but did not intend to spill the milk. Or even if they did intend to, it is not necessarily because they meant to be bad or naughty or to make extra work for their parent.

Blame can only be accurately placed on someone who intentionally (or deliberately, knowingly) causes foreseeable harm. Think of the distinction between murder vs manslaughter vs accident. In all of these cases, a behavior causes harm.

- However, with accidents there was no intention to cause harm and the behavior that caused harm was not done intentionally.
- In the case of manslaughter, the act that caused harm was done intentionally but there was no intention to harm or kill.
- Murder, on the other hand, does involve intention to harm and intentionally acting in a way that causes that harm.

So, if there is no intention, the person may be responsible but it is not accurate to blame them for what happened.

Similarly, confusing responsibility with causal responsibility often contributes to NAGS. Just because someone is accountable does not mean they have the power to control outcomes.

For example, let's say there's this great job. It pays $150,000 a year. Your job would be to make certain that everyone comes on time and that nobody leaves late. I could give you that job. And, I could hold you accountable and fire you if anyone comes late or leaves early. But, would you have the power to make certain that nobody comes late or leaves early? Would you really be responsible for each person's actions?

[Refer the client to the Responsibility section of the Workbook]

COMBAT/MILITARY ATROCITY GUILT EXAMPLE

[This is an example to use when someone did purposely cause harm.]

Sometimes, in the context of war, someone does something in the moment with intention to do harm. For example, going back into a village after a battle and killing more people. Again, consider the full context of this, including emotional states such as horror, rage, grief, or dissociation. In addition, just because one battle is over does not mean the threat is gone. In the context of war, a combatant is under chronic threat and therefore, in chronic survival (fight-flight-freeze) mode, so it is not surprising that the fight response continues even after one battle is won. What may come to seem ok in the context of war, doesn't feel ok anymore once back in the civilian world.

[Confusing causal responsibility with responsibility is very common for professionals in a protector role (e.g., leader in the military; police officer/first responders; doctors/ medical professionals). Because these roles are very strongly tied to a person's identity, the therapist should acknowledge the self-imposed and social expectations that accompany these roles.]

COMBAT/MILITARY EXAMPLE

A platoon leader could be held accountable for the deaths of troops in his unit and be court-martialed. But, did he have the power to keep everyone in his unit alive?

MEDICAL PERSONNEL EXAMPLE

A doctor takes an oath to do no harm and feels guilt after losing a patient. Is it possible to keep every patient alive?

Another thing that contributes to guilt is forgetting that most events have multiple causes. There are likely cultural variations on this. In Western culture, for example, we learn that individuals choose their own destiny as a matter of choice or free will and that we should accept responsibility for the consequences of our decisions. However, this conclusion does not take into account that most actions have multiple sources of causation and that situational and historical factors outside of ourselves exert a powerful influence on what we choose to do.

- Let's take the example of a pen rolling across the desk ***[demonstrate]***. What caused the pen to roll across the desk? To fall off my desk? Yes, obviously that I rolled it? What else? ***[If the client does not follow or can't think of any causes:]*** gravity, physics, the shape of the pen, etc.
- ***[Switch light on and off and ask:]*** What made the light go off and on? I flicked the switch, but what else? ***[Solicit and offer examples if the client does not follow or can't think of any other contributors, like:]*** the building is wired properly, Thomas Edison invented electricity and light bulbs, the property manager paid the bill, etc.

We tend to attribute responsibility mostly to causes that occurred closest to the event (e.g., me pushing the pen or flicking the light switch), although other factors contributed just as much, if not more.

- Think of the domino effect: If I push the first domino in a long row of dominos, who or what is responsible for the last one to fall? You might say that the second to last one is responsible for making the last one fall, but it only fell because the one before it pushed it over, and so on.... You might then say it was my all-powerful finger, but it didn't touch that last domino. And what if some of those dominos were missing or not placed properly? All of them are needed and in the proper place for it to happen. If you remove any one of them, the last one will not fall.

So, keeping that in mind, let's identify all the different contributors to your traumatic experience. What contributed to your traumatic event?

[Have the client turn to the Responsibility Analysis worksheet in their Workbook. Encourage the client to write down all of the people, factors, forces, and beliefs that contributed to the negative outcome that is the source of guilt. Once the client runs out of ideas, offer examples that you may have noticed in discussions with the client. You can also ask more questions about the trauma that might help you identify additional contributing factors.]

SEXUAL ASSAULT/ABUSE EXAMPLE

The colleague was very professional until the day of the assault; the perpetrator purposely manipulated the client to trust him and be alone with him; it is common to meet up with colleagues to discuss projects; it is normal for colleagues to say hello to each other; the perpetrator was stronger than the client; the perpetrator chose to assault/abuse the client; that the client was taught to be nice to everyone; that we live in a patriarchal society/culture; the freezing response.

COMBAT MILITARY EXAMPLE

Instructions given to the client by their commander that day; lives were at risk; what the client didn't know about the possible dangers in the situation; the training the client had received; the fact that the client was at war; in a combat zone or in actual combat (e.g., the context of the actual situation, chaos, fight-flight-freeze response); how tired the client was that day; how much sleep the client had in previous days; the information or lack of information the client had at that time; the chaos during the battle; the needs/expectations from the client's unit/the military; the rules of engagement; the military hierarchy; the enemy; enemies' actions; unit cohesion; the fact that the client's family was so proud the client was in the military; and the fact that the client didn't want to disappoint them.

SUICIDE EXAMPLE

The client's spouse had never mentioned suicide; or, had talked about it for years but never attempted it; or, always denied that she would ever do it; she had a history of depression for years without suicide attempt; she talked about the future; everything about that day/week seemed like every other day; she had mental illness; the presence of gun or pills; she declined help/therapy.

[Once the client has a thorough list of contributing factors, ask the client to go through the list and rate how much each factor contributed to the traumatic event from 0% to 100% (i.e., this can add up to more than 100%). Add up the percentages. Once the client has rated each factor, total them all up.]

So your rating of your responsibility on the AAGS was ____%. The total of all of the other contributing factors was __%.

If we were to make a pie chart, what would your piece look like in the whole pie?

[Add up all of the ratings and calculate the proportion of responsibility assigned to self, relative to total. For example, if the total percentage of all contributing factors is, for example, 480% and the client assigned 90% to their own action, then the actual proportion of responsibility assigned to them is 90/480 = 18.7%.]

So how does your responsibility compare relative to all of the contributing factors? Had you considered the big picture of the situation in this way before? What are your reactions to this?

Re-answer item #3 from the AAGS

So, let's review how you answered the question related to this on the AAGS. What is the answer that reality would dictate, that a judge and jury would conclude is the correct answer based on the evidence of what was the best option out of those you had at the time?

The first time you circled your answer. Now answer the item again, this time with a triangle around your answer.

You initially said you were ***[percentage given by the client]*** __ % responsible and now you say these other things are ***[sum of all percentages attributed to all other contributors identified by the client on worksheet]*** __ % responsible.

[Probe for uncorrected thinking errors and continue to address if needed.]

What is your reaction to the responsibility analysis?

[Continue to normalize if the client expresses that they still feel guilt and shame. It is important that the therapist does not force this process.]

4. Wrongdoing Analysis

Next, we will take a close look at what you think you did wrong. In other words, what personal or societal value(s) do you think you violated? This is another way we can experience guilt–we believe that we intentionally violated a value important to us. When you filled out the AAGS, what values did you believe you had violated?

[Refer the client to the Wrongdoing section of the Workbook.]

SEXUAL ASSAULT/ABUSE EXAMPLE
Caring for myself; protecting myself; protecting my children ***[e.g., in the case of domestic violence].***

COMBAT MILITARY/LAW ENFORCEMENT EXAMPLE
Valuing life; protecting/not harming others; not leaving anyone behind; being conscientious/dependable.

MEDICAL EXAMPLE
First, do no harm; save every life; conscientiousness/attention to detail.

SUICIDE EXAMPLE
Protecting/caring for my loved ones; being a good listener/there for others.

Recall that blame can only accurately be assigned as a label when someone intentionally causes foreseeable harm. Similarly, you can only accurately attribute wrongdoing to a person when they intentionally violate personal or societal values.

Another common thinking error is the tendency to conclude wrongdoing based on the tragic negative outcome rather than on the person's intentions or what they were trying to accomplish before the outcome was known.

Also, the circumstances in which trauma typically occurs are "Catch 22," "no-win," or "lose-lose" situations. Often, during a negative event, the options available in that moment are all suboptimal. In fact, often, they are all really lousy options. Not infrequently, every possible course of action is likely to lead to a bad outcome.

[Review Justification Analysis if relevant. "Remember what you realized in the justification analysis? That there were no good options, that there were reasons you made the choices you made."]

Some examples of situations where all outcomes can feel bad are: while in combat having to shoot an armed child; staying with an abusive spouse when you have no means financially to leave; not reporting your boss for sexual assault because you cannot afford to lose your job.

COMBAT MILITARY EXAMPLE

This type of dilemma is especially relevant to war. No doubt, sometimes none of your options are in line with the morals and values you may hold dear and can live by in the civilian world. The alternative you might have preferred does not actually exist in some contexts (e.g., leave and come up with a peaceful resolution). When this happens, we can experience a strong moral dilemma. The thinking error here is judging the dilemma based on peacetime morals and available options instead of on the actual available options and context, such as the rules of engagement.

It's also important to consider that we have multiple values at any given point in our lives, and the extent to which each one takes priority can change depending on the context and time of our lives. We will be talking a lot more about values in the next module.

- For example, a parent may have a value making sure their child always feels loved and cared for. They may also hold as values being a supportive and fair boss, being a hard worker, contributing to their community through volunteer work, etc. It is often not possible to prioritize every value at every given moment. Rather, they may prioritize their parenting values by spending quality time with their children when they are at home in the evenings, but may be focused on work when they are in a business meeting. This does not mean they don't still have that parenting value.

In sum, before you can make an accurate judgment about wrongdoing or violation of values, then, you need to recall what your motives were at the time. In other words, what values were you prioritizing, and what were the pros and cons of each of your available alternative courses of action at the time, which is not malicious or amoral.

During the traumatic event…

Did you intend to cause_________ **[the negative outcome]**?

Did you know what was going to happen when you ____________ ?

You see? Wrongdoing does not apply to you. [Optional: "Sorry. Not guilty. Case dismissed."]

[If there is a clear value that was being prioritized… . In fact, what you did was moral, in line with your value of ___________, wasn't it?**]**

Therapist Tips

A "yes" response to the intention question can be common for individuals that are experiencing ATROCITY GUILT. If the client reports that, yes, they did intend to cause the negative outcome, follow-up with some clarifying questions to better understand what led up to those actions and other contributing factors in the context in which the decision was made to act in that way.

Probe the emotional state at the time (e.g., strong anger and grief), and thoughts such as revenge and how the context (e.g., of war) affected that thinking.

Probe why they feel remorse now and if they believe they would truly do something like that now.

Did your emotional state have any influence on your behavior?

Were you under any kind of threat so that the fight-flight-freeze response was activated (whether you were aware of it or not at the time)?

How might what you did help alleviate some of the negative emotions or sense of threat you were experiencing?

Spotlight on Emotional Reasoning

Finally, emotional reasoning contributes to all of the different types of faulty guilt conclusions we might come to. Emotional reasoning is the belief that if we feel something then it must be true. For example:

"I feel guilty, therefore I must be guilty."

"I feel responsible, therefore I must be."

"I feel bad, therefore I must have done something wrong."

It's also important to remember that when something terrible happens like the trauma you experienced, everyone feels strong negative emotions, which we often just identify as feeling "bad." Often, we see that bad feeling as evidence that we did something really wrong—even that we must be responsible for what happened because we feel so bad. This is an "emotional reasoning" and is a kind of "circular logic."

It doesn't hold up when you look at it closely—feeling bad is not evidence of doing something bad. It's just a motivator to evaluate what happened to see what we might learn from it to keep from feeling bad in the future.

For example, feeling bad when someone close to us dies can prompt us to make more effort to spend quality time with those we love while they are still alive.

Re-answer item #4 from the AAGS

So, let's review how you answered the question related to this on the AAGS. What is the answer that reality would dictate, that a judge and jury would conclude is the correct answer based on the evidence of what was the best option out of those you had at the time?

The first time you circled your answer. Now answer the item again, this time with a triangle around your answer.

[Probe for uncorrected thinking errors and continue to address if needed.]

What is your reaction to this section?

[Again, allow space to process that the client may logically understand the difference but may not FEEL less guilty. Normalize this process and reinforce that their feelings may start to shift as the client continues to the guilt appraisal skills. It is important that the therapist does not force this process.]

> **Therapist Tips**
> Conduct additional guilt debriefings using a separate AAGS for additional guilt/shame thoughts related to trauma as needed prior to moving to the next module. These may be other thoughts from the same trauma or they may be thoughts related to a completely different trauma.
>
> If the client is not showing much movement with regard to how much they believe their guilt cognitions or how much they rate their guilt and shame after conducting a full appraisal of their most distressing guilt cognition(s), you may need to help them identify the function of holding on to their guilt, before moving on to appraising other guilt cognitions. See below ("What would it mean to feel less guilty going forward?") for strategies to help with this.

What would it mean to feel less guilty going forward?

[Have the client re-rate the remaining items on the AAGS.]

You've rated your beliefs about your guilt and how guilty you feel lower than you did at the beginning of this session. How does that feel? What would it mean to go forward in your life feeling less guilty?

Many people at this point in the treatment are not sure they want to give up their guilt even though they realize they are not as guilty as they have been telling themselves. Do you have any concerns about going on with your life feeling less guilty about this?

Therapist Tips

This discussion is intended to elicit beliefs about the pros and cons to going forward in life feeling less guilty. It is very important to bring the ambivalence about letting go of guilt and shame to the surface. When the clients believe the guilt is playing an important role in helping them live in accordance with values, they may hold on to the guilt and shame even after the debrief. Many clients will express thoughts such as, "If I feel less guilty then... I'm really a monster...what would keep me from doing bad things again... how would I honor the memory of the people I lost... it means I don't have control over it happening again, etc."

Here are strategies for addressing such thoughts:

- It sounds like the guilt has been serving an important function for you. Specifically, it has helped you live closely with a value that is clearly very important to you

  [Reframe the reasons the client identified for maintaining guilt into values—e.g., "it's very important to you to not hurt others... to honor the memories of people you've lost," "you respect yourself and want to do what it takes to protect yourself and your integrity," etc.].

- Although you have shared beliefs with me that you are not a very good person because of your role in the trauma [use the client's own words here], in fact you are someone who suffers greatly when you violate your values. Look at how much you have been suffering because you believed you violated a value that is important to you. Would an amoral or bad person suffer this much?
- Do you think there might be a way to express this value in your life other than suffering with guilt? Are you open to exploring this possibility with me?

Many times, guilt involves a loss of life of a close friend or family member and the client has come to believe that holding on to the guilt and shame is a way to preserve the memory of the departed. The following are additional potential strategies when guilt involves loss of life:

- Do a role reversal with the client pretending to be the person who died and having them contemplate whether they would want their friend/loved one to feel shame and guilt for the rest of their life, or whether they would want their friend/loved one to continue the rest of their life not feeling guilty about something they might have done.
- Ask if the client if they can think of other ways they might honor the memory of the person they lost.

Now that we see how deeply you hold your values, that you suffer so deeply with guilt and shame when you violate an important value, we are going to focus on identifying values that are important to you, not only ones affected by the trauma, but also all kinds of values, and we will help you find ways to live closely with them every day. We can't undo what happened during the trauma, but we can help you spend your time in ways that feel meaningful and in line with your values.

For every hour-long period all week, mark what activities you were doing. The easiest way to complete this is to check in with yourself at every meal time and then again at bedtime.

Homework Assignment

1. Evaluate each guilt thought on the Guilt and Shame Cognitions Log using the steps learned today.
2. Listen to the recording of this session at least one time.
3. Reread sections of the workbook discussed today.
4. ***[Only assign this once the client is done with the Guilt Appraisal Module (Module 2), which often takes two sessions]***: Complete an Activity Log for the week.
   Instructions: ***[Refer the client to first Daily Activity Log in their Workbook]*** For every hour-long period all week, mark what activities you were doing. The best way to do this is to work on this at every meal and record activities from the last few hours. Otherwise, it gets hard to remember what you were doing if you wait until the end of the day or near impossible if you wait until several days have passed. Let's write down today's activities up to now together to get you started. ***[Have the client fill in what they did today, including the therapy session.]***

Close the Session

- What is one thing you got out of today?
- What are your reactions to today's session?

[The following are some suggested questions you may ask to address any concerns about the treatment commitment or motivation.]

What might get in the way of you completing your homework or you coming back next week?

Why is this important to you?

What would happen if you dropped out?

What would be the pros and cons of engaging or not engaging in this treatment? What would be the worst thing that could happen if you stuck with this and kept trying?

End Session

MODULE 3: SESSIONS 5 AND 6

Commitment to living a value-driven life and setting value-driven goals

Session 5: Commitment to living a value-driven life and setting value-driven goals

In this module, the therapist helps the client identify their values, consider how their values may have been affected by the trauma, and work toward living a valued life. Although the topic of values can be vast, therapists are reminded to stay focused on the relationship between Nonadaptive Guilt and Shame (NAGS) and their client's value system.

[Ask client to start recording the session]

Review Homework

- Review Guilt and Shame Cognitions Log
- How did listening to the session go? What was it like to listen to the session? What struck you most as you listened to it?
- What were your thoughts about doing this therapy between the first session and today?
- Go over Daily Activity Log.

Trauma Informed Guilt Reduction Therapy
https://doi.org/10.1016/B978-0-12-814780-1.09983-4

Session Agenda:
1. Define values
2. How trauma affects values
3. What do you value?
   - o Retirement Party Exercise
   - o Values Worksheet
4. Approaching values with flexibility
5. Assign Homework
6. Close the session

Therapist Tips
During this session, you will ask the client to set goals on a blank activities sheet that is in their workbook. It is important to review the activities sheet they brought in today to understand how they are currently spending their time and where valued activities may fit. If the client did not complete their Daily Activity Log, prompt the client to try to fill in the log by memory.

1. Introduce values identification

Today, we are going to look at the ways that your guilt can help you live a more valued life. As a reminder guilt can be both nonadaptive and prevent you from living your life, and it can be adaptive and help you reconnect with your value system.

Tell me, how would you define values?

What are values?

Values are our foundation, our guiding principles. Your values can be thought of as your compass. Once you choose which direction you want to go, it's always there. The points/directions remain regardless of how you felt before and where you've been in the past, or how you feel and where you're headed now. North is always North. In each moment, you can choose to move in any direction.

You can spend time thinking about things that have occurred in the past that you are unhappy about or you could choose to follow the points on the compass that you have decided hold meaning for you. You can choose to do this despite what you were doing a moment ago or 5, 10, or 20 years ago.

Values are personal and acting on our values, living them, is what makes our lives meaningful.

We have values in many different life domains: relationships (romantic, family, friends, coworkers, roommates), work/career/vocation, training/education, recreation, well-being (mental health and physical health), financial, spiritual, environmental, community (volunteer, charity, political activity), etc.

And values can change...

- For example, what was important to you in a friendship when you were 5, 10, 18, 25, 40, etc.?

And, we can have many different values that take different levels of priority at different times. For example:

- Training and education values might be higher than financial ones while in college.
- Family-related values might be given precedence over work, career, or vocation-related values in times of family crisis.
- Financial values may be favored over values we might have about our vocation in times of acute hardship (e.g., you may not pass up the first promotion even though you are not really interested in that work and would rather wait for the next one).

2. Understand how values may be affected by trauma

The fact that you experience guilt means that you have values. You wouldn't feel guilty if you didn't think you acted against a value you held.

What are your thoughts about this?

Experiencing guilt following a trauma usually means you feel like you did something "wrong" or somehow violated a value that is important to you. So, while the guilt may not be accurate, it is still useful to pay attention to it. You can't do this if you're avoiding.

Tell me the ways you feel like your values were violated during your trauma? What values do you feel were affected by your experience?

Avoidance becomes overgeneralized. If we get in the habit of avoiding one thing, we can also start avoiding things we don't mean to, including awareness of our values and choosing to live according to them. So, we end up feeling more guilty. In other words, the more you avoid, the less you live according to your values. You might even find yourself moving in the opposite direction of things you value, that you act against values.

Example: Spending time with your children may be something you value, but you might not do it as much as you would like because of avoidance or guilt-related thoughts (e.g., I don't deserve to spend time with my kids because of what I did).

Instead, by not avoiding and working through trauma-related guilt, you can use guilt to help you live in line with your values.

Example: Someone who lost a loved one may say something like, "I feel guilty that I couldn't do more to protect the person I lost" and may identify the value that is important to them is taking care of those they care about. This thought process could help them get closer to the important people in their lives and ask themselves, "How can I take care of the people I love this week?"

As you have gone through this therapy, what have you noticed about how you want to live your life?

3. Identify values in different life domains

Let us spend some time discussing how you can connect with your values.

Reduce avoidance: pay attention to your guilt. Evaluate your guilt like we did in the last session(s) so that you don't have to continue to experience nonadaptive guilt and use your guilt to help identify important values.

Example: If a trauma involved seeing a child get hurt or killed, it may bring up an important value of not harming children or taking good care of children. Once you make note of that, you can think of things to do for your own child or for children in vulnerable situations (like volunteer work, choosing a career that helps children, or making a donation to a child-specific charity).

Recognize that while choices may have been limited during the traumatic event, choices are available for proceeding from this point forward.

There is nothing stopping you now from doing things in accordance with the value that was violated during your trauma.

Retirement Party Exercise

Let's explore your most deeply held values. I'm going to ask you to close your eyes and engage in a mindfulness exercise. Imagine yourself at an event celebrating you [e.g., your own Memorial Service/Retirement Party (use a retirement party if client becomes too uncomfortable thinking about their own funeral)] and imagine what you would like the guests to say about you. Not what you think they would say, but what you would really like to hear them say about what kind of person you are, the things you have done and said, and what you meant to them. Imagine your spouse, child(ren), closest friend(s), or coworkers and have them say what you would like them to say about you in turn. Now I'd like you to take a few moments to write down in your workbook some of the values that you identified during this exercise.

Introduce the Values Worksheet

[Start completing in session and assign the remainder of worksheet for homework.]

It is important to note that values do not have an end.

You can always be a better friend, partner, or family member. You can always be better to yourself.

Nor are values about outcomes.

Winning a "Mother of the Year" award is not a value, but wanting your kids to know how much you love and value them is.

Notice also that while some values complement one another very well, others can compete with one another

(e.g., You might want to pursue a satisfying and challenging career that does not include a high salary and this value might compete with the value of being financially independent)

What are some of the areas where you feel like your values have been neglected and you want to work on right now?

4. Approaching values with flexibility

Values are NOT commandments that we have to obey, or unrealistic standards that no human being can realistically meet.

Values often need to be prioritized and approached with flexibility. Because it is impossible to be in multiple places at once, you may have to choose which value to act on in a given moment. Priorities for different values may change overtime and be different in different contexts.

When you're in class you will probably prioritize education/training values and when you are on a date you will probably prioritize your intimate relationship values.

Someone who values being a loving and caring family member but also values being a hard worker may have to choose between meeting a work deadline and being at a family event.

Guilt can result from having to choose to act on one value over another.

But, choosing to act on one value in a moment does not mean that the other value ceases to exist. The next time you are in a similar situation you can make a different choice or you may be able to find a compromise. These are ways to approach valued situations with flexibility.

Guilt can also come up when people try to work on every value at once and set expectations for themselves that are impossible.

As you connect with values this week, how can you approach them in a way that does not set you up for disappointment?

Therapist Tips

Some clients may feel considerable guilt about feeling guilty (e.g., "What's wrong with me? Why do I feel guilty all the time?"). With these clients, it may be useful to discuss how guilt detracts from living life fully. It may help to suggest using one's energy for something meaningful and life-enhancing (i.e., values) rather than getting caught up in a vicious cycle of trying to make guilt go away, and then feeling badly for feeling guilt. In other words, it may help to encourage clients to be patient with themselves as they work to challenge guilt and to take values-guided action as a means of still living a meaningful life as this process unfolds.

Review the Activity Log completed for homework again, this time focusing on how activities fit into values:

What valued activities did you engage in this past week?

Where can you schedule valued activities/actions into your upcoming week? [***Work with the client to schedule valued activities from the Values Worksheet onto the Daily Activity Log***.]

How do you think participating in these might go?

Homework Assignment

1. Listen to the recording of this session at least one time.
2. Reread sections of the workbook discussed this week.
3. Continue to identify and evaluate guilt cognitions.
4. Continue work on the Values Worksheet.
5. Complete Daily Activity Log again and engage in planned value-driven activities.

Close the Session

- What is one thing you got out of today?
- What are your reactions to today's session?

[The following are some suggested questions you may ask to address any concerns about treatment commitment or motivation.]

What might get in the way of you completing your homework or you coming back next week?

Why is this important to you?

What would happen if you dropped out?

What would be the pros and cons of engaging or not engaging in this treatment? What would be the worst thing that could happen if you stuck with this and kept trying?

End Session

Session 6: A plan to live a valued life

[Ask the client to start recording the session]

Review Homework

- Review guilt challenging work.
- Review Values Worksheet
  - o Were you surprised by anything that came out during the Retirement Party, exercise, or any of the values you identified?
- Go over Daily Activity Log.
  - o How much time did you spend in activities related to any of these values this past week?
  - o What gets in the way of participating in valued activities?
- How did listening to the session go? (What was it like to listen to the session? What struck you most as you listened to it?)
- What were your thoughts about doing this therapy between the first session and today?

Session Agenda:

1. Goals for a value-driven life
2. Commit to living a value-driven life
   - o Steps to Living a Valued Life Worksheet
3. Complete final AAGS
4. Treatment planning if needed
5. Conclude Trauma Informed Guilt Reduction (TrIGR)

1. Develop goals to live a valued life

Today, we are going to continue to focus on values. Let's review why we are focusing on values in this treatment about guilt and shame.

What is your understanding of why we are spending time on this?

We've seen over the last few weeks that you violated deeply held values during the trauma. Unfortunately, you cannot undo the past. However, you can make choices about the future. That is what we are going to focus on for the remainder of the therapy. How do you employ your values to help you live a meaningful, satisfying life going forward.

[NOTE: Introduce Steps to Living a Valued Life worksheet. You and the client will work through this worksheet through Step 3 below.]

Today, we will focus on finding ways to bring your values more into your life every day as a way to work toward this goal. First, we will start by having you identify some specific ambitions that fall within each value area (family, work, etc.) that we reviewed during the last session. What domain would you like to start with?

[Go through several or all areas of the worksheet with the client.]

Therapist Tips

Refer client to the worksheet listing domains in the workbook. Give an example from your client's own life regarding goals they may want to set. If they are struggling, you can use the example string given below, but preferably use their own example.

Example: Training/education value: to learn a trade that will allow me to support my family while doing work I enjoy.

Ambitions:

A. Complete a master's degree in social work
B. Learn how to conduct therapy that helps Veterans with their problems
C. Find work in a setting that helps Veterans
D. Treat Veterans

As you reach for each ambition, you may have different specific goals:

A. Identify Master's programs in social work and apply
B. Study for and pass grad school entrance exams
C. Maintain a certain GPA in grad school
D. Get an internship in a setting that treats Veterans

To achieve each goal, you may have to first break it down into smaller steps.

For the goal of identifying Master's programs in social work, there are a number of steps you must first take:

A. Do an internet search of programs
B. Talk to a social worker who is a Veteran
C. Visit top choice programs
D. Talk to current students and faculty at top choice programs

Note that a number of steps are usually involved in setting goals themselves.

In order to talk with current students and faculty, you may need to take some of the following steps:

A. Make a list of what you are looking for in a program
b. Make a list of questions you would like to ask
C. Draft an email to send to people asking to talk with them

Overcoming obstacles to meeting goals

It is not uncommon for things to get in the way of meeting our goals. We can have the best intentions to live closer to the value of taking care of health by making a goal to exercise, but then we don't get to the gym. Has this ever happened to you? Thinking ahead about what might get in your way and how you will overcome it will up the chances that you will meet your goal. For example, if I try to go to the gym after work but I'm always tired then, I can try going at a different time of day.

Therapist Tips

Spend time helping clients think of obstacles that may get in the way of their ability to work toward their goals. At this stage in treatment, many clients have confidence in their abilities to live a better life. Although this is a positive step for clients, it is important to help prepare them for obstacles that life will invariably throw at them. Make sure clients list obstacles and steps to overcome them in the appropriate spaces on the Steps to Living a Valued Life worksheet.

Important reminders about values

Living with your values is a lifelong process. We're never done. It's not something we achieve or complete. It's not like, "Okay, I've lived that value, now I'm done with it."

Our values can change throughout the course of our lives. And some can take priority over others at any given moment. We get to choose if we are not avoiding.

Moving toward ambitions and goals and taking steps that are in line with your values will bring meaning to life. The meaning in values is in acting on them, not the outcome of our actions.

***[Present skiing metaphor*:]** The goal of skiing is getting down the mountain in good shape, but the fun is in getting down there, maneuvering the moguls, falling and getting back up, feeling the wind and rush, etc. Skiing would have no meaning if you took an elevator down to the bottom.

Besides, there is a lot that is not in your control. So, it would be unrealistic for the meaning of life to be at the mercy of outcomes.

- You may set a goal of spending more time with an important loved one and make specific plans to make it happen, but they have an emergency and are not available that week. You still took the steps to live with your values even though the outcome was not what you had hoped.

Reviewing the Values Worksheet again

Make sure the valued life domains, goals, and actions are feasible, notice that while values have no end, specific goals and steps do.

Keep asking yourself, "What is this ambition, goal, step in the service of and will this action, if taken, actually produce the goal or help lead to it?"

Make sure there are plenty of small, achievable steps that have the potential to present quick positive results. The impact of taking little steps consistently is generally greater than big heroic steps done inconsistently.

The emphasis is on doing actions that feel like "steps in the right direction" (i.e., actions taken that are experienced as consistent with the client's values and stated goals).

2. Commit to living a valued life!

Scheduling is an important part of leading a value-driven life. Thinking about your values, ambitions, goals, and the steps you might take doesn't bring meaning, but acting on them does. What step(s) do you want to schedule into your week/month/year?

Remember that you always had and always will have a compass. And that it does not matter which direction you were heading in the previous moment, you can always choose to move in your valued direction this moment, and the next. It doesn't matter if you were heading in a non-valued direction for 5, 10, or 15 years, you always had and continue to have your compass. This is your foundation. This is you.

> **Therapist Tips**
> This initial work on identifying and committing to living one's values is just that: initial. Encourage clients to continue this work.

3. Closing therapy, continued treatment planning

We have spent several weeks identifying the sources of your guilt and shame, examining them closely to understand what values you felt were violated, and identifying ways you can live with those values you hold closely in the future.

What have been the biggest changes for you over the last few weeks?

Are there changes in how you understand your guilt?

Are there changes in your feelings of guilt?

What are important next steps for you?

How will you continue down this road?

In what areas do you feel you still need work? Guilt? Other PTSD symptoms? Functional difficulties? Let's talk about your next steps of treatment. You have worked very hard the last few weeks, asked yourself very difficult questions, and confronted very painful feelings and memories. It was extremely brave of you to do this and I hope that you, your family, and the people closest to you reap the rewards of your work for a long time to come.

> **Homework Assignment**
> 1. Reread the sections of the workbook discussed this week.
> 2. Listen to the recording of the session at least once.
> 3. Continue to identify and evaluate guilt cognitions.
> 4. Continue working on the Values Worksheet and Steps to Living a Valued Life worksheet.
> 5. Complete the steps you have scheduled.
> 6. Follow-up on the treatment plan you have made with your therapist if you are continuing therapy.

End Session

Optional for Module 4: Making amends

Some clients may conclude that it is important to them to make amends or take reparative action. Note that this rarely comes up and is rarely needed. Making the commitment to behave (from this point forward) in accordance with one's values can in and of itself be reparative and/or make amends.

Clients may generate some of the following ideas:

1. Apologize for wrongdoing (to victim, through confession, etc.).
2. Share information with loved ones of people that died during trauma.
3. Become a better parent by enrolling in parenting classes, reading books, talking with children, or entering family therapy.
4. Continue with rescue/aid work.
5. Create something good from the circumstances.
6. Build memorials.
7. Train/inform others in coping/dealing with future trauma.
8. Take social action (e.g., raising public awareness, volunteer, and listen to a friend in need).
9. Pursue justice, accountability (not for one's own sake, but for that of the law/justice).

The therapist's goals are to:

1. Explore with the client the value underlying this intent, the function it will serve, and whether this is the best option for how to express this value.
2. Help clients understand that they can take action but it may not have their desired outcome (e.g., they may apologize but the recipient may not accept the apology). Is the client ok with going through the process although the outcome is not known?
3. Help the client consider the impact their action may have on the recipients of their amends. Might it cause pain or harm to anyone?

PART 4

Client workbook

Introduction to posttraumatic guilt and shame

Introduction to the Workbook

Welcome to your Trauma Informed Guilt Reduction (TrIGR) therapy Workbook. The goal of TrIGR is to help you feel less guilt, shame, and distress from your trauma and to help you live the life you want to live. Your workbook is organized to follow along with what you are doing in therapy.

You will be using this workbook in each TrIGR session with your therapist and throughout the week in between sessions, so it is best to keep it with you while you are completing this treatment. We encourage you to take notes, write questions, highlight, ear-mark, and otherwise use the manual in any way that is most helpful. If you like, you can also share the material with loved ones to help them understand what you are doing in the treatment.

A Note About Examples: Throughout the workbook, we present examples to help illustrate some points. We have purposefully selected the most common examples that are applicable to different kinds of trauma, as well as some that capture unique aspects of some types of trauma. Please note, we do not assume that any or all examples will apply to you or any particular person. Your therapist may offer other examples that are more relevant to your own experiences.

Audio-recording and between session homework: It is sometimes hard to take in all of the information the therapist is presenting in session since you are processing your own thoughts and reactions (sometimes strong emotional reactions) at the same time. For this reason, your therapist will ask you to audio-record your meetings and listen to the recording before you meet again. There are prompts (i.e., [Start Recording]) in this workbook at the beginning

Trauma Informed Guilt Reduction Therapy
https://doi.org/10.1016/B978-0-12-814780-1.09997-4

of each session to help remind you of this. You will also be asked to practice skills you learn in therapy in between sessions. Practicing the skills is one of the most important parts of this treatment. In fact, research has shown that practice outside of therapy sessions is one of the most important predictors of benefiting from therapy. Your therapist will explain practice assignments at the end of each session and your workbook has instructions for each practice assignment.

Session 1: Overview of TrIGR, Introduction to Guilt and Shame

[Start recording]

Session Agenda:
1. TrIGR format and content
2. Guilt, shame, and their relationship with posttraumatic distress
3. Why guilt and shame are common following trauma
4. Homework assignment

1. Introduction to TrIGR

What can you expect from this treatment?

You and your therapist will meet approximately 4–7 times, for up to 90 min each time, and you will be asked to complete practice assignments between sessions. Your therapist will ask you to record your meetings and listen to the recording at least once in between your meetings. During the therapy, you will talk about guilt and shame following trauma with your therapist, you will go through a series of exercises to more fully process your own trauma memories and emotions, and you will work toward a future where you live a value-driven life (i.e., the life you want to live), with goals and activities that feel meaningful and consistent with your values.

Each session will follow a similar format in a similar order. Specifically, you will:

1. Review homework assignments
2. Learn and practice new concepts and skills
3. Discuss new homework assignment
4. Share feedback and questions

Today's meeting will focus on understanding why feelings of guilt and shame are common after trauma.

2. Understanding guilt and shame and its relationship to trauma

The following are extremely common experiences following a traumatic event:

- Guilt: Feeling distress because you think you should have thought, felt, or acted differently.
- Shame: Feeling bad about yourself.
- Anger: Feeling distress because you think you or someone else should have thought, felt, or acted differently.
- Loss/Grief: Feeling distress because you lost friends or loved ones, or even belongings. Some losses after trauma can be symbolic, such as the loss of identity, your former self, or your former life before the trauma, innocence, self-worth, faith in God or human nature, optimism, sense of control, and/or values and meaning.

Why do we focus on guilt and shame?

The following are frequent sources of distress and pain after trauma.

- A car accident survivor may feel guilty that someone else was hurt.
- A domestic violence survivor may feel guilty for having stayed in the relationship or allowing children to witness the abuse.
- A sexual assault survivor may feel guilty for not having been able to stop the assault.
- A family member may wish they could have stopped their loved one from committing suicide.
- A first responder who couldn't save an injured person.
- A military Veteran who may have done things, seen things, or made decisions that have life and death consequences, and/or may have been unable to stop things that go against their core values.

You may develop a sense of having gone so far against your values that you will never see yourself, others, or the world in the same way again. In this therapy, we refer to this as trauma-related guilt and shame. Sometimes this is called "moral injury."

Feeling guilty may also be a way of taking control again after experiencing a trauma, the very definition of which includes loss of power and control. When a trauma occurs, the world can feel unpredictable and blaming yourself for what happened can be a way of making it predictable again. Saying "it's my fault" is sometimes an attempt to convince oneself that you can stop it from happening again.

In some cases, someone is dependent on the person who is traumatizing them. For example, someone who is abused may not have the ability to leave right away. Blaming oneself (e.g., "The abuse is my fault") can be a way to maintain a relationship with a perpetrator when that is critical for survival.

Unfortunately, while it makes sense that guilt is a common reaction after trauma, there is a cost. Guilt can make symptoms and distress after trauma worse and keep people from recovering:

- The distress you feel when you think about what you should have done differently during the trauma can cause you to avoid thinking about the trauma. This interferes with "processing" the trauma emotions and memories which is an important part of recovery.
- Left unchallenged, conclusions you have drawn about your role in the trauma or its aftermath (e.g., "It's my fault, I should have ______, I must have deserved it …") start to seem like facts.
- When people feel guilty but don't examine it, the guilty feeling can spread to all areas of their lives and they may experience shame about who they are as a person. They may have beliefs such as "I am a bad person."
- People experience shame when guilt thoughts such as "I did something bad" become thoughts like "I am bad." They may believe "I am unlovable." They may think, "I don't deserve to feel better."

Beliefs like these can negatively affect many areas of a person's life, such as the ability to feel close to family or other loved ones. They can keep people from living the life they want to live.

3. Why are Guilt and Shame Common After Trauma?

One reason people experience guilt is that it can be adaptive. It can help us learn from our experiences and figure out if there is anything we might do differently the next time we are in a similar situation.

- For example, if you are really rushed one morning and end up yelling at your loved one to hurry up, you may feel guilty later. If you take the time to analyze why you feel guilty, you may decide, "that's not the kind of person I want to be in this relationship. What can I do differently next time?" You may decide to apologize and to wake up a little earlier or get some things ready the night before from now on.

Another way guilt can be adaptive is that it serves as a beacon, shining a light on what is important to us, what our values are.

- For example, a parent who missed their child's softball game may feel guilty. Examining why they feel guilty, they might find that being there for their child's games is very important to them and can prompt them to make a commitment to do things differently in the future, such as changing their schedule so they can make their child's big games in the future.

Finally, guilt may prevent us from acting in a way that violates our personal and/or societal values. It's an unpleasant feeling to say the least, so we want to avoid feeling it.

- For example, someone tells his best friend he will take him out on his birthday but when the night comes, does not feel like going out. Because the person values being a good friend, he may choose to take his friend out anyway, to live according to his value of being a good friend.

Guilt becomes a problem when we don't have the opportunity to realistically evaluate and learn from what happened or take steps to make things better. What often happens instead is we start believing the story that our guilt/distress tell us; we buy into it (e.g., "I feel guilty therefore I must have done something terribly wrong"). When we buy into it in this way, we give up the chance to find out if we really could have done something differently and/or guilt may turn to shame (e.g., "I did something bad so I must be a bad person").

When this happens, guilt and shame can intensify, increase distress, and interfere with many aspects of life.

Why is it difficult to use guilt adaptively after trauma?

When something as terrible as a traumatic event occurs, it is very difficult to make sense of why it happened. It is very common for people to blame themselves and tell themselves that if they had just made a better choice they would have been able to prevent the bad outcome.

There are also aspects of traumas and the contexts in which they occur that can make it more likely that they will lead to guilt and shame. For example:

- If you were trained to believe that you were responsible for the lives of others (e.g., troops under your command or patients under your care).
- If you were abused by someone you were dependent on and had to maintain a relationship with that person.
- If you were not able to process the emotions from your trauma for a long time because you had to deal with more pressing issues (e.g., ongoing danger, lives still at risk).

Another major contributor to guilt and shame becoming a problem is *avoidance.*

- Because guilt is a very unpleasant feeling, it is common to avoid thinking about the guilt or the event that caused you to feel guilty. Avoidance does not allow us to learn from a situation or to evaluate whether or not a conclusion about guilt is accurate.
- Avoidance keeps people stuck in a cycle of feeling bad because they believe they did something wrong which leads to feeling even worse. Feeling worse leads to even stronger beliefs of "I should have done something differently" which leads to feeling even worse and so forth.
- We call this *Nonadaptive Guilt and Shame, or NAGS* for short.

How Do We Treat NAGS?

Guilt consists of feelings and thoughts. We will focus primarily on thoughts. In order to do so, we will look at different aspects of what happened during your trauma. In this way, we will take a more direct look at what happened in a way that is less overwhelming than if we were to try to address all of the feelings and thoughts at once.

Homework Assignment

1. Reread sections of the workbook discussed this week.
2. Listen to the recording of the session at least once.
3. Write down any questions or concerns you have about the therapy and bring these to the next session.

Session 2: Common Problems and Types of Guilt Related to Trauma

[Start recording]

Session Agenda:
1. Trauma reactions and common problems
2. Types of trauma-related guilt
3. Your experience with trauma-related NAGS
4. Assign Homework

1. Trauma Reactions: Posttraumatic Stress Disorder (PTSD), Depression, Substance Use

A traumatic event is a situation in which someone's life, your own or someone else's, is at risk. Common examples of traumatic experiences include combat, physical and sexual assaults, witnessing someone die or almost die, car accidents, and natural disasters like fires, floods, and earthquakes.

What are common problems after a traumatic event?

Most people feel very upset after a trauma. They may think about the trauma even when they do not want to, may have a hard time calming down, or they may feel depressed. They may drink or use drugs more than usual, or engage in other distracting activities to try to deal with their feelings after the trauma.

For many people, these problems get better after a couple of months, but for many, they continue.

When these problems do not go away after a few months, they can become PTSD, depression, or a substance use disorder.

What is Posttraumatic Stress Disorder (PTSD)?

PTSD consists of four types of symptoms:

- *Intrusive* symptoms are thinking about the trauma even when trying not to. This can be in the form of memories, images, nightmares, or even flashbacks.
- *Avoidance* symptoms involve not only avoiding the trauma memory, but also people, places, and activities that are reminders of the trauma.
- *Negative changes in thoughts and mood* can include feelings of guilt and shame as well as anger, fear, grief, loss of interest in activities that used to be enjoyable, and having a hard time feeling close to others.
- *Arousal* symptoms can include trouble sleeping, trouble concentrating, and feeling on guard, keyed up or on edge.

What is Depression?

- Feeling down or depressed is very common following a traumatic event. This may be related to grief or loss if the trauma involved the death of someone close to you. Some people also report feeling like they have lost a part of themselves. It may also be related to having difficulty resuming your usual activities and feeling as if life has lost some of its meaning.
- Depression can be a part of PTSD but it can also be a separate problem, especially when it is accompanied by difficulty sleeping, loss of interest in activities you used to enjoy, changes in appetite/weight, low energy/motivation, feelings of worthlessness, and frequent thoughts of death or that you would be better off dead. For some people, these symptoms can last for weeks or even months, making it very hard to function.

What is a Substance Use Disorder?

- Drinking alcohol or using other drugs is common following trauma. Sometimes people drink or use other drugs in order to get to sleep, be around people more easily, or to quiet the distressing memories and thoughts in their minds. This is called "self-medication."
- Substance use may be a way to avoid thinking about trauma or feeling difficult trauma-related emotions.
- Sometimes drinking or drug use can be a form of self-punishment.
- For some people, what may be helpful in the short run can turn into a problem of its own. Substance use can lead to many negative consequences (e.g., legal, relationship, social, or health problems) and, most importantly, it *interferes with recovery from trauma-related problems*, including guilt and shame.
- Signs of a substance use disorder include the following:
    1. Using more or for longer period than intended
    2. Wanting to cut down/stop but not being able to
    3. Spending a lot of time obtaining the substance, using, or recovering
    4. Cravings and urges to use the substance
    5. Not keeping up with work, school, home responsibilities
    6. Continued use despite relationship problems
    7. Giving up important activities due to substance use
    8. Repeated use in risky/dangerous situations
    9. Continued use despite physical or psychological problems
    10. Needing to use more to get the same effect (tolerance)
    11. Withdrawal symptoms (depending on the substance)
- Substance use can cause problems even if it is not a disorder.

Who is at risk of developing mental health problems or suffering after trauma?

It is not clear why some people develop problems like PTSD, depression or substance use after trauma while others do not. A few things do seem to put people at higher risk for experiencing problems and distress.

One of these risk factors is avoidance. Avoidance of the trauma memories and reminders such as certain people and places keeps people from processing trauma emotions like sadness and guilt and from learning that they can handle the avoided situations.

Another risk factor is certain ways of thinking about the world or oneself after the trauma. These thoughts might be about:

- Your reaction: *I failed, I should have done more. I was paralyzed and that means I'm a failure. I felt nothing and that means I'm a monster. I didn't report it, so that must mean I wanted it to happen.*
- Your role in it: *It was my fault. I should have been able to stop it. I should have known this was going to happen.*
- What it means about you, others, the world, the future: *I am evil, I am damaged goods or defective, people are evil and cannot be trusted, I let people down, the world is dangerous and no one can be counted on.*

Fight-Flight-Freeze During Trauma Can Lead to Guilt and Shame

During life threatening events, it is natural for animals, including humans, to go into fight, flight, or freeze responses. We review these briefly here because they often come up when we process traumatic events in the next part of this therapy. That is, some of the things people feel guilty about may be due to a fight, flight, or freeze response.

- Fight: stay and face the threat
- Flight: escape
- Freeze: lose ability to respond, sometimes physically freeze

Our brains are hardwired to do whatever it takes to survive a life-threatening situation and this survival mechanism will hijack the thinking part of your brain to deal with the threat quickly and expertly, regardless of how we might feel about it later.

Sometimes people feel guilty about their response during a traumatic event. "I should have done more," "I should have fought harder. Instead I froze." Or "I ran away. I let people down." However, this may not have been a choice someone made, but rather their fight, flight, or freeze response kicking in. This is an example of how what people tell themselves about a traumatic event can lead to guilt and shame.

2. Common Types of Trauma-Related Guilt and Shame/NAGS

There are many different ways that people experience guilt related to a trauma they experienced. Some of these might apply to you and others likely will not.

a. **Negligence/betrayal/abandonment guilt:** Behaving negligently (e.g., neglecting or not doing one's job, falling asleep when on patrol or at the wheel) or not doing more in a situation. Two underlying assumptions of this kind of guilt are that: (1) you were capable of doing more and thus should have done more, and (2) what you actually did was not effective.

b. **Incompetence/superman/superwoman guilt:** Believing that you can control uncontrollable physiological responses, like the fight, flight, or freeze response. Underneath this kind of guilt is a belief that you should have been able to make everything right, you should have been able to save the day. This type of guilt can occur when one's actions were impacted by fear, honest mistakes, accidents, inexperience, or inadequate training.

c. **Survivor or leaving guilt:** Feeling guilt for living when someone else died or leaving a dangerous situation when others had to stay behind. Medical personnel can experience this kind of guilt when someone dies in their care.

d. **Feeling pleasure or nothing during the trauma:** War Veterans will sometimes tell us they feel guilt and shame because they felt pleasure at the moment they killed someone. In fact, this is a common physiological response. When someone's life is in danger and then the danger is removed, the body can release hormones that feel like a rush of pleasure. Another example of this kind of guilt is among sexual assault survivors. When body parts involved in sex are touched, it is normal to feel arousal, even if the touch is unwanted. This can produce a lot of confusion and shame. Some people describe feeling betrayed by their body.

e. **Atrocity guilt:** This can occur when someone observes or participates in a terrible or horrific act against another human being. Because such an act is so wrong and unjustifiable under normal circumstances, it leads someone to come to the conclusion that their entire character must be flawed. Usually, the person feeling guilty does not take into account that even humane (i.e., kind and compassionate) people with high standards for themselves can behave inhumanely under certain conditions.

f. **Self-blame to maintain an important relationship:** It is common to place blame on oneself in order to be able to maintain a relationship with someone who has some power and control. For example, abused children often believe they are being abused because they did something wrong. It is easier for them to maintain attachment to their parent on whom they depend for food, a home, etc., if they blame themselves for the abuse instead of the parent.

g. **Not reporting the assault (or other crime against you or someone else):** This is a common source of guilt in physical or sexual assault survivors who believe they could have prevented future assaults to themselves or others. What the survivor typically is not recalling is all of the reasons why they did not, or could not, take action.

3. Your Experience with Guilt

Use the **Guilt and Shame Cognitions Log** that follows to write down the thoughts you are having when you notice feelings of guilt or shame. Jot down anything that seems related to guilt as close as possible to when you are experiencing or thinking about it.

Here are some common guilt-related beliefs people have about traumatic experiences:

- I should have known better.
- I should/shouldn't have done/said…
- Why did/didn't I…?
- I had no reason to…
- I did something wrong when I…
- It's my fault that … happened, because I …
- I don't deserve anything good because...
- I deserved [the trauma, or other bad things] to happen.

Homework Assignment

1. Reread sections of the workbook discussed this week.
2. Listen to the recording of this session at least once.
3. Identify and list guilt cognitions on the log. Try to do this each day.
4. Jot down any thoughts, questions, and concerns you have about the therapy, the readings, and the assignments, so that you can go over them with your therapist at your next session.

Guilt and Shame Cognitions Log

When you find yourself feeling guilt or shame, write down:

1. Your thoughts at the time (e.g., "I failed someone, I didn't do well enough, I'm evil…").
2. A sentence or two about specific situations you are feeling guilty about (e.g., "When I realized my friend was injured").

Debriefing the traumatic event and appraising trauma related guilt and shame

Sessions 3 and 4: Guilt Appraisal

[Start recording]

> **Session Agenda:**
> 1. Examine guilt in a systematic way
> 2. Explore how guilt has helped you express important values
> 3. Homework assignment

Once you and your therapist have selected a guilt event to work on today, complete the questionnaire below.

Trauma Informed Guilt Reduction Therapy
https://doi.org/10.1016/B978-0-12-814780-1.09996-2

Attitudes About Guilt Survey (AAGS)

People who have experienced traumatic events often experience guilt related to these events. They may feel guilty about something they did (or did not do), about beliefs or thoughts they had (that they now believe to be untrue), or about having had certain feelings (or lack of feelings).

The purpose of this questionnaire is to evaluate how you feel about ONE (and only one) guilt issue at a time. Please complete a separate AAGS for each guilt issue you have.

Please take a moment to think about your experience. Briefly describe what happened:

____

____

____

I should have/shouldn't have (*circle one*):

____

In answering each of the following questions, please circle ONE answer that best describes your view of what happened.

1. To what extent do you think you should have known better and could have prevented or avoided the outcome?
   a. There is no possible way that I could have known better.
   b. I believe slightly that I should have known better.
   c. I believe moderately that I should have known better.
   d. For the most part I believe that I should have known better.
   e. I absolutely should have known better.

2. How justified was what you did? (i.e., How good were your reasons for what you did?)
   a. What I did was completely justified (excellent reasons).
   b. What I did was mostly justified.
   c. What I did was moderately justified.
   d. What I did was slightly justified.
   e. What I did was not justified in any way (very poor reasons).

3. How personally responsible were you for causing what happened?
   a. I was in no way responsible for causing what happened.
   b. I was slightly responsible for causing what happened.
   c. I was moderately responsible for causing what happened.
   d. I was largely responsible for causing what happened.
   e. I was completely responsible for causing what happened.

   On a scale of 0%–100%, how responsible were you for what happened: ______ %
4. Did you do something wrong? (i.e., Did you violate personal standards of right and wrong by what you did?)
   a. What I did was not wrong in any way.
   b. What I did was slightly wrong.
   c. What I did was moderately wrong.
   d. What I did was very wrong.
   e. What I did was extremely wrong.

5. How distressed do you feel when you think about what happened?
   a. I feel no distress when I think about what happened.
   b. I feel slightly distressed when I think about what happened.
   c. I feel moderately distressed when I think about what happened.
   d. I feel very distressed when I think about what happened.
   e. I feel extremely distressed when I think about what happened.

6. Circle the answer which indicates how often you experience guilt that relates to what happened.

   Never Seldom Occasionally Often Always

   Whenever I think about it

7. Circle the answer which indicates the intensity or severity of guilt that you typically experience about what happened.

   None Slight Moderate Considerable Extreme

A systematic way of examining guilt and shame

Guilt is a mix of feelings and thoughts. Today's goal is to work on thoughts. Specifically, we will focus on four kinds of guilt thoughts to get a fuller picture of what happened during your trauma.

1. Foreseeability and Preventability (Hindsight Bias)
2. Insufficient Justification
3. Causal Responsibility
4. Violation of Values (Wrongdoing)

The way you remember an event can lead to faulty conclusions about your role in the trauma.

1. Foreseeability and Preventability: Believing that you knew the trauma was going to happen and therefore should have been able to prevent it

Hindsight bias: When knowledge of how an event turned out (e.g., who won a football game) distorts or biases a person's memory of what (s)he knew before the outcome was known. Hindsight-biased thinking often happens when someone says "I should have known better…I should have done something differently … I saw it coming…I knew what was going to happen."

Hindsight bias is an important concept because it often applies to how we judge our actions leading up to a traumatic event. After a trauma, many survivors falsely believe they knew what was going to happen, which leads them to believe they could have prevented what happened.

Of course, there are sometimes red flags, or signs or a hunch, that something bad might happen. But these are rarely the only pieces of information available at the time. We typically have many pieces of information to consider when making decisions. In reality, acting on hunches rarely pays off. For example, "My team hasn't won in a long time, maybe today is their day" doesn't mean it will pay off to bet your life savings on your team today. If your team does finally win today, that is not evidence that you should in fact have bet your life savings, because most likely you would have lost it!! Also, we usually only remember the red flags and rarely ever remember all the green flags (all the reasons we had to do what we did).

If you are feeling guilty because you think you knew what was going to happen and failed to prevent it, ask yourself this million dollar question:

If you knew with certainty what was going to happen when you did what you did, would you have done what you did?

If the answer is "No," that is proof you did not know what was going to happen. And, therefore, you are not guilty of not having prevented it.

2. ***Lack of Justification: Believing that you did not have good reasons for actions you took or did not take.***

   You might come to this inaccurate conclusion if you are…

   a. …weighing the benefits of actions you took against actions you thought of later that weren't actually possible at the time.
   b. …weighing the choices you made against choices that you didn't think of until much later.
   c. …focusing only on "good" things that might have happened had you done something else.
   d. …not considering the context in which you had to make the decisions you did.
   e. …not considering the good things that came out of the choices you did make. For example, you survived.
   f. …using information you know now to evaluate the pros and cons of options you had at the time (hindsight bias). At the time you made the decisions you made, you didn't know how things would turn out, so it's not fair (or accurate) to judge those decisions as if you did.

Let's think about this. You may not have had the luxury to take time to make your decision. We all may make different decisions when we have little time and are in danger (when fight-flight-freeze has kicked in) than when we have the time to weigh out all the pros and cons.

Once you perceive a threat, the fight-flight-freeze response gets activated and you only have three options: fight, flight, or freeze. And your survival mechanism will select which one is optimal for your survival, regardless of how you might feel about it later.

Justification Analysis Worksheet

What options did you have and consider at the time of your trauma? And what were the pros and cons for each of these options during the trauma?

	Pros:	Cons:
Option A		
Option B		
Option C		
Option D		
Option E		

Was there actually a good choice?
Which option was the best choice (or least bad choice)?

3. ***Responsibility: How much responsibility you place on yourself versus all of the other factors that played a role in the trauma and confusing responsibility with blame.***

   a. Confusing responsibility with blame. Consider knocking over a glass of water by accident versus purposely dumping a glass of water on someone.

   b. Confusing responsibility in terms of being accountable ("This is my job to do") with responsibility in terms of having the power to cause or control outcomes.

   c. Not taking into account all of the forces that caused the traumatic events (consider the domino effect).

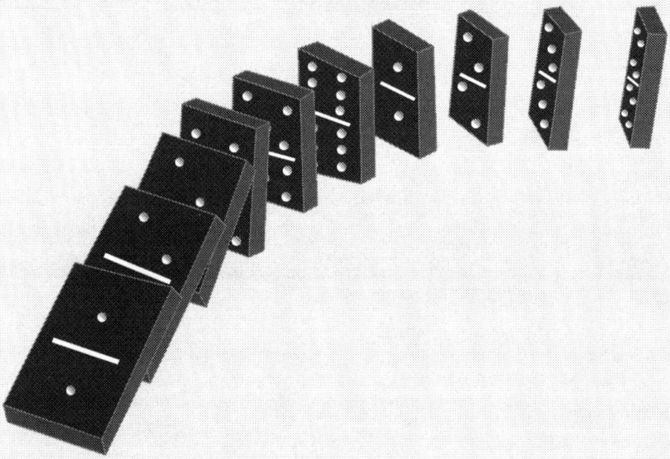

Responsibility Analysis

How responsible are you for what happened?

Who or what else contributed to the traumatic event?

%	Contributory Factor
	Grand Total Percentage

Your % ______ ***Total %*** ______

4. *Wrongdoing: Concluding that you violated your or society's values*

Common thinking errors that lead people to believe they did something wrong include the following:

a. Incorrectly assuming intentionality (or deliberateness).

b. Concluding there was wrongdoing based on what happened rather than based on your intentions before you knew what would happen.

c. Not recognizing that in some situations, the least bad choice is the best choice.

d. Judging the situation based on your or society's standards you have the luxury of living up to when you are not in a stressful situation or under threat and not considering the context in which you had to act.

e. Not considering that the survival response might have been activated, which means you would only have the three options of fight, flight, or freeze available to you and which one your survival brain selected was not up to you.

f. Forgetting that all people have multiple values and that sometimes you have to prioritize one over another. For example, you may value your career and your family and sometimes you have to make a choice of one that is not ideal for the other. This does not mean other values do not matter to you. It also means you were acting according to your values, even if not all of them.

Spotlight on: Emotional Reasoning

This is a type of thinking that contributes to all the different types of faulty conclusions we might come to. Emotional reasoning is the belief that if we feel something it must be true. For example:

"I feel guilty, therefore I must be guilty."

"I feel responsible, therefore it must be my fault."

"I feel bad, therefore I must have done something wrong."

"I feel shame, therefore there must be something wrong with me."

Homework Assignment

1. Evaluate each guilt thought on your Guilt and Shame Cognitions Log using the steps learned today.
2. Listen to the recording of today's session at least once.
3. Reread sections of the workbook discussed this week.
4. If you are starting Module 3 next session, complete the Daily Activity Log for the week.
   Instructions: for every hour-long period all week, mark what activities you were doing. The easiest way to complete this is to check in with yourself at least at every meal time and then again at bedtime.

Attitudes about Guilt Survey (AAGS) (extra)

[This AAGS is to debrief a second trauma. Print more copies as needed for additional traumas.]

People who have experienced traumatic events often experience guilt related to these events. They may feel guilty about something they did (or did not do), about beliefs or thoughts they had (that they now believe to be untrue), or about having had certain feelings (or lack of feelings).

The purpose of this questionnaire is to evaluate how you feel about ONE (and only one) guilt issue at a time. Please complete a separate AAGS for each guilt issue you have.

Please take a moment to think about your experience. Briefly describe what happened:

____

____

____

I should have/shouldn't have (*circle one*):

____

In answering each of the following questions, please circle ONE answer that best describes your view of what happened.

1. To what extent do you think you should have known better and could have prevented or avoided the outcome?
   a. There is no possible way that I could have known better.
   b. I believe slightly that I should have known better.
   c. I believe moderately that I should have known better.
   d. For the most part I believe that I should have known better.
   e. I absolutely should have known better.

2. How justified was what you did? (i.e., How good were your reasons for what you did?)
   a. What I did was completely justified (excellent reasons).
   b. What I did was mostly justified.
   c. What I did was moderately justified.
   d. What I did was slightly justified.
   e. What I did was not justified in any way (very poor reasons).

3. How personally responsible were you for causing what happened?
   a. I was in no way responsible for causing what happened.
   b. I was slightly responsible for causing what happened.
   c. I was moderately responsible for causing what happened.
   d. I was largely responsible for causing what happened.
   e. I was completely responsible for causing what happened.

   On a scale of 0%–100%, how responsible were you for what happened: ______ %
4. Did you do something wrong? (i.e., Did you violate personal standards of right and wrong by what you did?)
   a. What I did was not wrong in any way.
   b. What I did was slightly wrong.
   c. What I did was moderately wrong.
   d. What I did was very wrong.
   e. What I did was extremely wrong.

5. How distressed do you feel when you think about what happened?
   a. I feel no distress when I think about what happened.
   b. I feel slightly distressed when I think about what happened.
   c. I feel moderately distressed when I think about what happened.
   d. I feel very distressed when I think about what happened.
   e. I feel extremely distressed when I think about what happened.

6. Circle the answer which indicates how often you experience guilt that relates to what happened.

   Never Seldom Occasionally Often Always

   Whenever I think about it

7. Circle the answer which indicates the intensity or severity of guilt that you typically experience about what happened.

   None Slight Moderate Considerable Extreme

Daily activity log

	Monday	Tuesday	Wednesday	Thursday	Friday	Saturday	Sunday
6–7 AM							
7–8							
8–9							
9–10							
10–11							
11–12							
12–1 PM							
1–2							
2–3							
3–4							
4–5							
5–6							
6–7							
7–8							
8–9							
9–10							
10–11							
11–12							
12–3 AM							
2–5 AM							
5–6 AM							

MODULE 3, SESSIONS 5 AND 6

Commitment to living a value-driven life and setting value-driven goals

Session 5: Commitment to living a value driven life and setting value driven goals

[Start recording]

Session Agenda:

1. Define values
2. How trauma affects values
3. Reconnecting with values
4. Approaching values with flexibility
5. Homework assignment

1. What are values?

Values are like the points on a compass. They are always there and each moment you can choose to move in their direction or not. Regardless of where you were going the moment before, or for the past 5, 10, or 20 years.

Values are as individual as our fingerprints. They are what make us tick and living them is what makes our lives meaningful.

The fact that you experience guilt means that you have values. You wouldn't feel guilty if you didn't think you acted against a value you held.

Trauma Informed Guilt Reduction Therapy
https://doi.org/10.1016/B978-0-12-814780-1.09995-0

We have values in many different areas of life: relationships (romantic, family, friends, coworkers, roommates), work/career/vocation/training/education, recreation, well-being (psychological, physical), financial, spiritual, environmental, community (volunteer, charity, political activity), etc.

Actual values or how we prioritize them can change over time and in different circumstances.

2. How are values affected by trauma?

Guilt and shame are signs that a value was violated.

When you avoid thinking about the trauma, you can lose track of what you value. You might find yourself even move in the opposite direction of your values, or act against your values, and then you may feel even more guilt and shame.

Working through guilt and shame as you have been doing is a step toward reconnecting with important values.

3. How can I reconnect with my values?

Reduce avoidance: pay attention to your feelings, including when you have felt guilty or ashamed in the past.

Recognize that while choices may have been limited during the traumatic event, choices are available going forward.

Remember, you violated a value during the trauma, but nothing is stopping you from honoring that value now.

4. Approaching values with flexibility

This past week you tracked how you spent your time. Today, you and your therapist will set goals for how you will spend some of your time this coming week. As you reconnect with values this week, remember that values are not commandments that we have to rigidly obey, or unrealistic standards that no human being can realistically meet.

Remember—it is impossible to be in multiple places at the same time! Because of this, values often need to be prioritized in each circumstance.

Be flexible with yourself and remember that values don't cease to exist if you choose one over another. And what you choose can vary from day to day.

Homework Assignment

1. Listen to the recording of this session at least once.
2. Reread sections of the workbook discussed this week.
3. Continue to identify and evaluate guilt cognitions.
4. Complete the Values Worksheet.
5. Complete the Daily Activity Log again and engage in planned value-driven activities.

Your retirement party

Imagine yourself at an event celebrating you and imagine what you would like your guests to say about you. Not what you think they would say, but what you would really like to hear from them say about what kind of person you are, the things you have done and said, and what you meant to them. Imagine your spouse, child(ren), closest friend(s), and coworkers and write below what you would like them to say about you.

Values worksheet instructions

Below are different values domains. Not everyone has the same values and this worksheet is not a test to see if you have the "correct" values. You may even choose to leave some areas blank because they are lower priority for you right now. Try to describe your values as if no one would ever read this worksheet. As you work, think about each area in terms of both concrete goals you might have and also in terms of more general life directions.

For example, you might value getting married as a concrete goal and being a loving spouse as a valued direction. The first example, getting married, is something that could be completed. On the other hand, the second example—being a loving spouse—does not have an end. You could always be more loving, no matter how loving you already are. Work through each of the life domains.

1. **Family relations.** In this section describe the type of brother/sister, son/daughter, father/mother you want to be. Describe how you want to be in these relationships and how you want to treat your family members.

   ____
   ____
   ____
   ____

2. **Friendships/social relations**. What does it mean to you to be a good friend?

   ____
   ____
   ____
   ____

3. **Marriage/couples/intimate relations**. In this section we would like you to write down a description of the person you would like to be in an intimate relationship. Write down the type of relationship you would want to have. Try to focus on your role in that relationship.

   ____
   ____
   ____
   ____

4. **Employment**. In this section describe what type of work you would like to do. This can be very specific or very general. After writing about the type of work you would like to do, write about why that appeals to you. Next, discuss what kind of worker you would like to be with respect to your employer and coworkers. What would you want your work relationships to be like?

____

____

____

____

5. **Education/training**. If you would like to pursue an education, formally or informally, or to pursue some specialized training, write about that. Write about why this sort of training or education appeals to you.

____

____

____

____

6. **Recreation**. Discuss the type of recreational life you would like to have, include hobbies, sports, leisure activities, etc.

____

____

____

____

7. **Spirituality**. What we mean by spirituality is whatever that means to you. This might be as simple as communing with nature, or as formal as participation in an organized religious organization. If this is an important area of your life, write about what you would want it to be like.

____

____

____

____

8. **Volunteer work/charity/political activities**. How would you like to contribute to your community (volunteer work, participation in local government, or a community group focused on conservation or other issues)?

____

____

____

____

9. **Physical well-being**. What do you value in regard to your physical well-being? Write about health-related issues such as sleep, diet, exercise, smoking, etc.

____

____

____

____

10. **Psychological, emotional**. What would you like to accomplish in therapy? What are important ways to take care of yourself?

____

____

____

____

Daily activity log

	Monday	Tuesday	Wednesday	Thursday	Friday	Saturday	Sunday
6–7 AM							
7–8							
8–9							
9–10							
10–11							
11–12							
12–1 PM							
1–2							
2–3							
3–4							
4–5							
5–6							
6–7							
7–8							
8–9							
9–10							
10–11							
11–12							
12–2 AM							
2–5 AM							
5–6 AM							

Session 6: A plan to live a valued life

[Start recording]

Session Agenda:
1. Goals for a value-driven life
2. Commit to living a value-driven life
3. Concluding TrIGR

1. Develop goals to live a valued life

Things to remember about values

Living your values is a lifelong process. You're never done. Your values can change throughout the course of your life and some can take priority over others at any given moment. You get to make choices about what's important if you are not avoiding.

Moving toward ambitions and goals and taking steps that are in line with your values will bring meaning to your life. The meaning of them is in acting on them, not the outcome of those actions.

- For example, the goal of skiing is getting down the mountain in good shape, but the fun is in getting down there, maneuvering the moguls, falling and getting back up, feeling the wind and rush, etc. Skiing would have no meaning if you took an elevator down to the bottom.

There is a lot that is not in your control. It would be unrealistic for the meaning of your life to be at the mercy of outcomes.

- For example, you may set a goal of spending more time with an important loved one and make specific plans to make it happen, but they have an emergency and are not available that week. You still took the steps to live your values even though the outcome was not what you had hoped.

2. Commit to living a valued life!

Scheduling is an important part of leading a value-driven life. Thinking about your values, ambitions, goals, and the steps you might take doesn't bring meaning, but acting on them does. What step(s) do you want to schedule into your week/month/year?

Remember that you always had and always will have a compass. And that it does not matter which direction you were heading in the previous moment, you can always choose to move in your valued direction this moment, and the next. This is your foundation. This is you.

3. Closing therapy, planning for the future

You have worked very hard, asked yourself very difficult questions, and confronted painful feelings and memories. It was extremely brave of you to do this work and we hope that you, your family, and the people closest to you reap the rewards of your work for a long time to come.

Are there areas that you still need to work on? Talk to your therapist about next steps in your treatment if desired.

Homework Assignment

1. Reread sections of the workbook discussed this week.
2. Continue to identify and evaluate guilt cognitions.
3. Continue working on Values Worksheet and Steps to Living a Valued Life.
4. Complete the steps you have scheduled.
5. Follow-up on the treatment plan you have made with your therapist if you are continuing therapy
6. Listen to the recording of this session.

Congratulations! This concludes your TrIGR therapy.

Steps to living a valued life worksheet

Complete one of these for each value you identified in each of the life domains the Values Worksheet. Some people find it easier to complete each heading group in turn, that is, list all your ambitions under the one value you are working on first. Then list all of the specific goals for each ambition, and then identify some steps you can take to move toward each goal.

Life Domain (e.g., family relationships, employment, etc.):

____

Value: ______________________________________

Ambitions (what, generally, would you like to achieve within this life domain that fits with your values?):

Ambition #1 ________________________________

Goals (what, more specifically, would you like to do in this area?):

Goal #1 ________________________________

Steps (what are some little things you can start doing now to move toward achieving your goals?):

Step 1: ______________________________
Step 2: ______________________________
Step 3: ______________________________

Goal #2 ________________________________

Steps (what are some little things you can start doing now to move toward achieving your goals?):

Step 1: ______________________________
Step 2: ______________________________
Step 3: ______________________________

Goal #3 ____________________

Steps (what are some little things you can start doing now to move toward achieving your goals?):

Step 1: ____________________
Step 2: ____________________
Step 3: ____________________

What might get in the way of meeting these goals?

What can you do so that doesn't happen?

Ambition #2 ____________________

Goals (what, more specifically, would you like to do in this area?):

Goal #1 ____________________

Steps (what are some little things you can start doing now to move toward achieving your goals?):

Step 1: ____________________
Step 2: ____________________
Step 3: ____________________

Goal #2 ____________________

Steps (what are some little things you can start doing now to move toward achieving your goals?):

Step 1: ____________________
Step 2: ____________________
Step 3: ____________________

Goal #3 ____________________

Steps (what are some little things you can start doing now to move toward achieving your goals?):

Step 1: ____________________
Step 2: ____________________
Step 3: ____________________

What might get in the way of meeting these goals?

What can you do so that doesn't happen?

Ambition #3 ________________________________

Goals (what, more specifically, would you like to do in this area?):

Goal #1 ________________________________

Steps (what are some little things you can start doing now to move toward achieving your goals?):

Step 1: ________________________________
Step 2: ________________________________
Step 3: ________________________________

Goal #2 ________________________________

Steps (what are some little things you can start doing now to move toward achieving your goals?):

Step 1: ________________________________
Step 2: ________________________________
Step 3: ________________________________

Goal #3 ________________________________

Steps (what are some little things you can start doing now to move toward achieving your goals?):

Step 1: ________________________________
Step 2: ________________________________
Step 3: ________________________________

What might get in the way of meeting these goals?

What can you do so that doesn't happen?

Daily activity log

	Monday	Tuesday	Wednesday	Thursday	Friday	Saturday	Sunday
6–7 AM							
7–8							
8–9							
9–10							
10–11							
11–12							
12–1 PM							
1–2							
2–3							
3–4							
4–5							
5–6							
6–7							
7–8							
8–9							
9–10							
10–11							
11–12							
12–2 AM							
2–5 AM							
5–6 AM							

Attitudes about Guilt Survey (AAGS)

People who have experienced traumatic events often experience guilt related to these events. They may feel guilty about something they did (or did not do), about beliefs or thoughts they had (that they now believe to be untrue), or about having had certain feelings (or lack of feelings).

The purpose of this questionnaire is to evaluate how you feel about ONE (and only one) guilt issue at a time. Please complete a separate AAGS for each guilt issue you have.

Please take a moment to think about your experience. Briefly describe what happened:

____

____

____

I should have/shouldn't have (*circle one*):

____

In answering each of the following questions, please circle ONE answer that best describes your view of what happened.

1. To what extent do you think you should have known better and could have prevented or avoided the outcome?
   a. There is no possible way that I could have known better.
   b. I believe slightly that I should have known better.
   c. I believe moderately that I should have known better.
   d. For the most part I believe that I should have known better.
   e. I absolutely should have known better.

2. How justified was what you did? (i.e., How good were your reasons for what you did?)
   a. What I did was completely justified (excellent reasons).
   b. What I did was mostly justified.
   c. What I did was moderately justified.
   d. What I did was slightly justified.
   e. What I did was not justified in any way (very poor reasons).

3. How personally responsible were you for causing what happened?
   a. I was in no way responsible for causing what happened.
   b. I was slightly responsible for causing what happened.
   c. I was moderately responsible for causing what happened.
   d. I was largely responsible for causing what happened.
   e. I was completely responsible for causing what happened.

   On a scale of 0%–100%, how responsible were you for what happened: ______ %

4. Did you do something wrong? (i.e., Did you violate personal standards of right and wrong by what you did?)
   a. What I did was not wrong in any way.
   b. What I did was slightly wrong.
   c. What I did was moderately wrong.
   d. What I did was very wrong.
   e. What I did was extremely wrong.

5. How distressed do you feel when you think about what happened?
   a. I feel no distress when I think about what happened.
   b. I feel slightly distressed when I think about what happened.
   c. I feel moderately distressed when I think about what happened.
   d. I feel very distressed when I think about what happened.
   e. I feel extremely distressed when I think about what happened.

6. Circle the answer which indicates how often you experience guilt that relates to what happened.

   Never Seldom Occasionally Often Always

   Whenever I think about it

7. Circle the answer which indicates the intensity or severity of guilt that you typically experience about what happened.

   None Slight Moderate Considerable Extreme